CROSS STITCH
WORLD OF ANIMALS

CROSS STITCH
WORLD OF ANIMALS

OVER 50 EXCLUSIVE DESIGNS

HELENA TURVEY

HAMLYN

To my husband Raymond and to my son Alex, who both have given me so much support during the making of this book, and to our much loved animals of past and present, Manda, Lucy, Suki, Lady, Bruno and Honey.

CROSS STITCH WORLD OF ANIMALS

Helena Turvey

First published in 1998 by Hamlyn
an imprint of Reed Consumer Books Limited
Michelin House, 81 Fulham Road
London, SW3 6RB
and Auckland and Melbourne

Publishing Director LAURA BAMFORD

Executive Editor SIMON TUITE
Editor ALISON BOLUS

Art Director KEITH MARTIN
Art Editor LISA TAI

Special Photography by DEBI TRELOAR
Cut out Photography by VICTORIA GOMEZ
Illustrations by CAROLYN JENKINS
Chart artwork by RAYMOND TURVEY

Production JULIE HADDINGHAM

The publishers have made every effort to ensure that all instructions given in this book are accurate and safe, but they cannot accept liability for any resulting injury, damage or loss to either person or property whether direct or consequential and howsoever arising. The author and publishers will be grateful for any information which will assist them in keeping future editions up-to-date.

A CIP catalogue for this book is available from the British Library.

ISBN: 0 600 59420 3

Produced by Toppan Printing Co Ltd
Printed and bound in China

Contents

Foreword

All the different regions of the world – from polar snows to arid deserts, mountain ranges to grasslands, and tropical forests to deep oceans – have their own characteristic wildlife, whose coats or markings reflect the part of the world they inhabit. The tiger's stripes provide camouflage as it stealthily stalks its prey through the undergrowth of tropical forests; the chameleon's skin changes colour to blend into its surroundings, and the subtly marked seahorse finds a natural disguise in seaweed and rocks.

The variety of shapes, sizes, textures and colours in the animal kingdom is amazing, and it can produce a wealth of ideas for embroidery designs. Some animal markings are strong and bright and so are easy to use for a design; take, for example, the zebra with its stripes, the leopard with its distinctive spots, or the parrot with its bright and primary-hued plumage. Other animals have

more subtle markings, not obvious at first glance but there if you look closely. The armadillo's leathery coat contains many shades of earthy colours, and the strange, jointed construction of its body makes an interesting design in itself.

Through researching design material for *Cross Stitch World of Animals*, I realized how many of our animals are on the verge of being lost forever, either through our own greed or through pure ignorance. One example is the lemurs on the island of Madagascar, whose habitat is fast disappearing as the tropical forests are burnt down for crop production. Another example is the effect that domestic pets, brought in by immigrants, have had on the rare flightless birds found in New Zealand. On the positive side, however, there are many people who are aware of what is happening and who are trying to help save the animal kingdom. By spreading this awareness, we can all contribute to these animals' safety.

The enjoyment and interest I have had from researching the projects in this book were enhanced by my recent discovery that, during the 1920s, my great great aunt Edith courageously travelled and worked as a midwife on her own through South America, Africa and Asia, from where many of these animals originate.

CARDS AND PICTURES

Most of the designs in this chapter can be interchanged into either cards or pictures. The deer card could be framed to hang on the wall with the Siberian tiger, and the tropical fish could be used for summery greetings cards. Frames can be embroidered too, to enhance a mirror or special photograph.

Panda Birthday Card

The strong markings of the giant panda make a dramatic contrast with the soft green bamboo leaves.

Measurements

The finished embroidery size is 8.2 x 8cm (3¼ x 3⅛ in).

Materials

- Piece of antique white 16-count Zweigart DMC Aida measuring 20 x 20cm (8 x 8in)
- DMC or Anchor stranded embroidery cotton, one skein of each colour shown on the chart
- Tapestry needle size 24-26
- 15cm (6in) embroidery hoop
- White oval-framed embroidery gift card, size 15.5 x 11cm (6⅛ x 4½in)
- Glue or double-sided sticky tape
- Basic sewing kit

To work the embroidery

Following the chart, start your embroidery from the centre of the markings you have placed on your Aida fabric (see page 101). Work the cross stitches with two strands of embroidery thread. When you have completed the cross stitching, work the details of the bamboo in back stitch, using one strand of DMC 319/Anchor 1044 for the outline of the bush and leaves and two strands for the bamboo stems. Next work the outline, eyes and nose of the panda in back stitch, using one strand of DMC 310/Anchor 403, and finally sew one long stitch for the centre of each eye, using two strands of DMC B5200/Anchor 1.

Treat the finished embroidery (see page 101), then mount the embroidery in the gift card, following the instructions on page 104.

	DMC	Anchor
	700	228
	703	238
	760	1023
	310	403
	823	152
	930	1035
	B5200	1
	746	386

Back stitch

	DMC	Anchor
	319	1044
	310	403

Wapiti Deer Christmas Card

The wapiti deer of North America use their impressive antlers to battle for control of the herd.

Measurements

The finished embroidery size is 12.5 x 12.5cm (5 x 5in).

Materials

- Piece of navy blue 18-count Zweigart DMC Aida measuring 25.5 x 25.5cm (10 x 10in)
- DMC or Anchor stranded embroidery cotton, one skein of each colour shown on the chart
- Tapestry needle size 24-26
- 20cm (8in) embroidery hoop
- Blue square-framed embroidery gift card, size 20 x 15cm (8 x 6in)
- Glue or double-sided sticky tape
- Basic sewing kit

To work the embroidery

Following the chart, start your embroidery from the centre of the markings you have placed on your Aida fabric (see page 101). Work the cross stitches with one strand of embroidery thread. When you have completed the cross stitching, work the details of the deer, rocks and trees in back stitch, using one strand of DMC 310/ Anchor 403; the grass in long stitch, using one strand of DMC 3345/Anchor 263 and the stars in long stitch, using one strand of DMC 5282 (Anchor has no gold thead).

Treat the finished embroidery (see page 101),

then mount the embroidery in the gift card, following the instructions on page 104.

	DMC	Anchor
■	310	403
▨	822	885
▦	436	1045
▢	842	388
▨	840	393
▨	434	370
□	644	830
▨	647	8581
◪	844	1041
▨	827	159
▨	341	117
◪	828	9159
□	B5200	1
⌐	B 5200	1

Long stitch

	DMC	Anchor
▨	3345	263
■	5282	–

Kyushu Crane Mirror Frame

These elegant and subtly coloured cranes – with their blue-grey feathers, white napes and flashes of red – decorate the border of a mirror beautifully.

Measurements

The finished embroidery size is 19 x 13.5cm (7½ x 5¼in).

Materials

- Piece of cream 16-count Zweigart DMC Aida measuring 38 x 38cm (15 x 15in)
- DMC or Anchor stranded embroidery cotton, one skein of each colour shown on the chart
- Tapestry needle size 24-26
- 20cm (8in) embroidery hoop
- Photograph frame of your choice
- Basic sewing kit

To work the embroidery

Following the chart, start your embroidery from the centre of the markings you have placed on your Aida fabric (see page 101). Work the cross stitches with two strands of embroidery thread. When you have completed the cross stitching, work back stitch where shown, using one strand of DMC 310/Anchor 403, and work a French knot for each eye, using one strand of the same thread.

To treat finished embroidery, see page 101.

To make up the frame

Tack the central position of the embroidery in one coloured thread and the position in which the mirror will be in another. (Note that the central position of the embroidery is not the centre of the mirror. The mirror will be placed in the space left within the embroidery design and should be in a central position to the surrounding frame.) Take it to a professional framers to be framed.

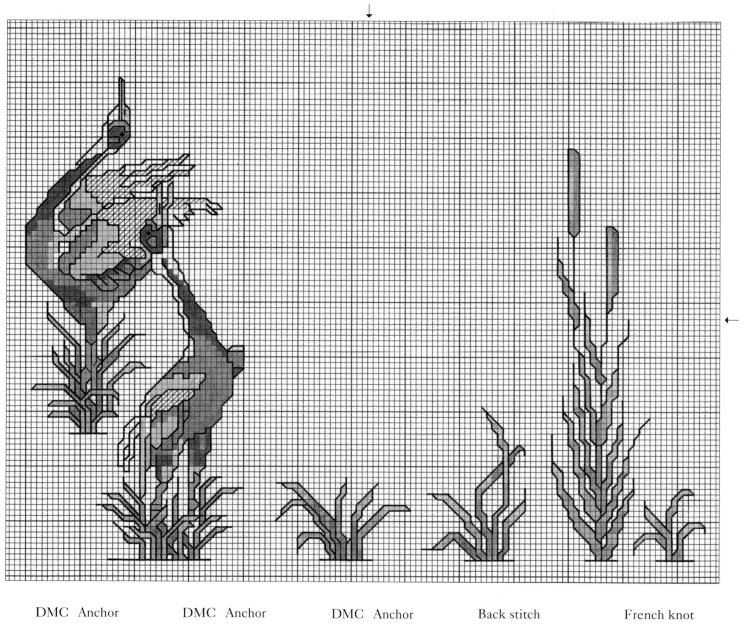

	DMC	Anchor		DMC	Anchor		DMC	Anchor	Back stitch		French knot	
	644	830		825	979		3756	1037	DMC	Anchor	DMC	Anchor
	310	403		B5200	1		3761	9159	310	403	310	403
	3705	35		518	1039		369	1043				
	451	233		792	177		368	261				
	761	894		932	976		367	210				

Siberian Tiger Picture

The dignity, poise and dramatic markings of this tiger make it the perfect subject for a picture.

Measurements

The finished embroidery size is 10 x 5cm (4 x 2in).

Materials

- Piece of cream 18-count Zweigart DMC Aida measuring 20 x 20cm (8 x 8in)
- DMC or Anchor stranded embroidery cotton, one skein of each colour shown on the chart
- Tapestry needle size 24-26
- 15cm (6in) embroidery hoop
- Picture frame
- Acid-free mounting board
- Strong thread for stretching embroidery

To work the embroidery

Following the chart, start your embroidery from the centre of the markings you have placed on your Aida fabric (see page 101). Work the cross stitches with one strand of embroidery thread. When you have completed the cross stitching, work the tiger's outline and face details in back stitch, using one strand of DMC 310/Anchor 403, then use the same thread to sew the whiskers in long stitch.

To treat the finished embroidery, see page 101.

To frame the picture

Mount the picture following the instructions on page 104 and then frame it, or have it done professionally at a framers.

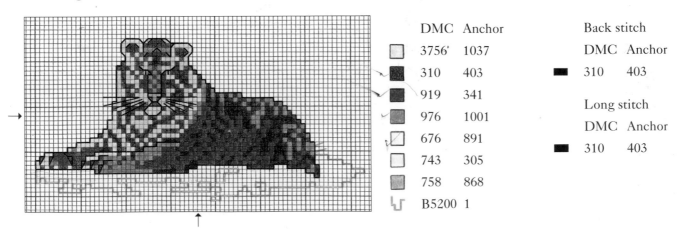

	DMC	Anchor
	3756	1037
	310	403
	919	341
	976	1001
	676	891
	743	305
	758	868
	B5200	1

Back stitch

	DMC	Anchor
	310	403

Long stitch

	DMC	Anchor
	310	403

Butterfly Photograph Frame

The tiger butterfly is so called because of its stripy markings and colouring.

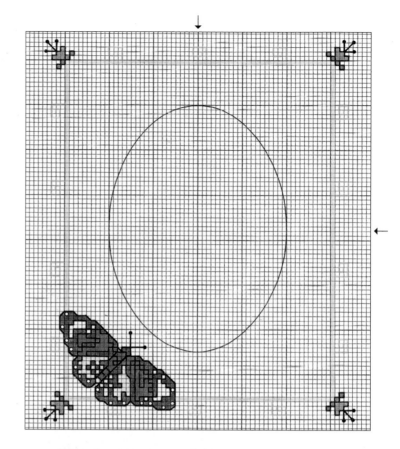

Measurements

The finished embroidery size is 11 x 13cm (4⅜ x 5⅛in).

Materials

- Piece of cream 16-count Zweigart DMC Aida measuring 24.5 x 25.5cm (9⅝ x 10in)
- DMC or Anchor stranded embroidery cotton, one skein of each colour shown on the chart
- Tapestry needle size 24-26
- 20cm (8in) embroidery hoop
- Photograph frame of your choice with a minimum inner frame measurement of 12 x 14cm (4¾ x 5½in)
- Basic sewing kit

To work the embroidery

Following the chart, start your embroidery from the centre of the markings you have placed on your Aida fabric (see page 101). Work the cross stitches with two strands of embroidery thread. When you have completed the cross stitching, sew round the butterfly and flowers in back stitch, using one strand of DMC 310/Anchor 403, then work the centre of the flowers in long stitch. Sew the antennae in back stitch, using two strands of the same thread. Work French knots as follows: for the flower centres using one strand of DMC 310/ Anchor 403; for the antennae using two strands of this thread, and round the wings using one strand of DMC Blanc/Anchor 2.

Sew round the border in back stitch, using one strand of DMC 988/Anchor 257. Treat the finished embroidery (see page 101).

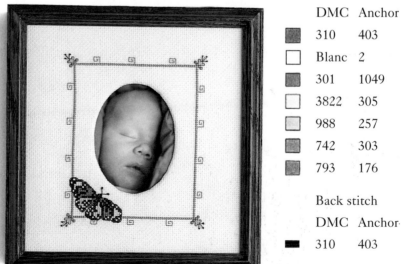

	DMC	Anchor
■	310	403
□	Blanc	2
▨	301	1049
▢	3822	305
▨	988	257
▨	742	303
▨	793	176

Back stitch

	DMC	Anchor
▬	310	403

To make up the frame

Follow the instructions on page 105 then have it framed.

Four Tropical Fish Pictures

The Hawaiian Islands have many brightly coloured tropical fish living in their coral reefs.

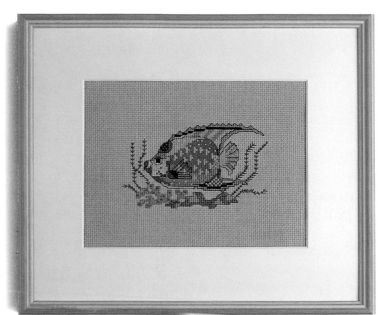
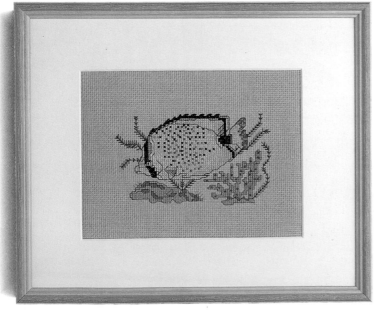
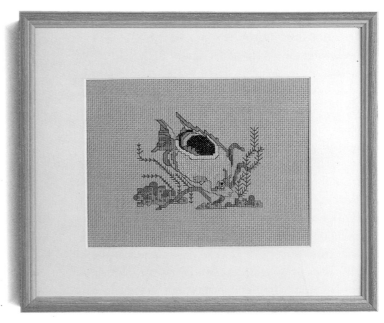

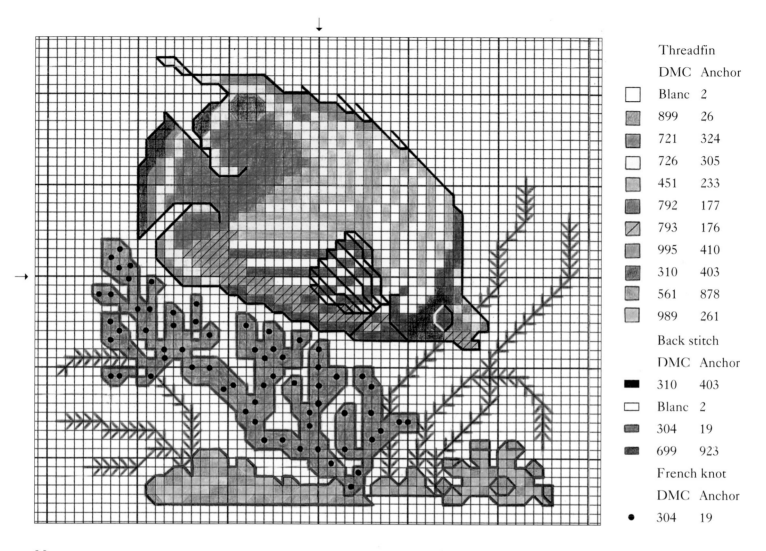

Threadfin

DMC	Anchor
Blanc	2
899	26
721	324
726	305
451	233
792	177
793	176
995	410
310	403
561	878
989	261

Back stitch

DMC	Anchor
310	403
Blanc	2
304	19
699	923

French knot

DMC	Anchor
304	19

Measurements

The finished embroidery size varies with each fish:
Threadfin 11 x 9cm (4¼ x 3½in)
Queen angel 13.5 x 8cm (5⅜ x 3⅛in)
Milletseed 14.5 x 8.5cm (5¾ x 3¼in)
Saddleback 11.7 x 9cm (4⅝ x 3½in)

Materials

• Piece of sea-green 14-count Zweigart DMC Aida measuring
  27 x 27cm (10½ x 10½in) for each picture
• DMC or Anchor stranded embroidery cotton, one skein of
  each colour shown on the charts
• Tapestry needle size 24-26
• 15cm (6in) embroidery hoop
• Acid-free board to fit frame of choice (x 4)
• Strong thread for stretching embroidery
• Masking tape

To work the embroidery

Following the chart, start your embroidery from the centre of
the markings you have placed on your Aida fabric (see page
101). Work the cross stitches with two strands of embroidery
thread. When you have completed the cross stitching, follow
the instructions given overleaf, depending on which fish you
are working.

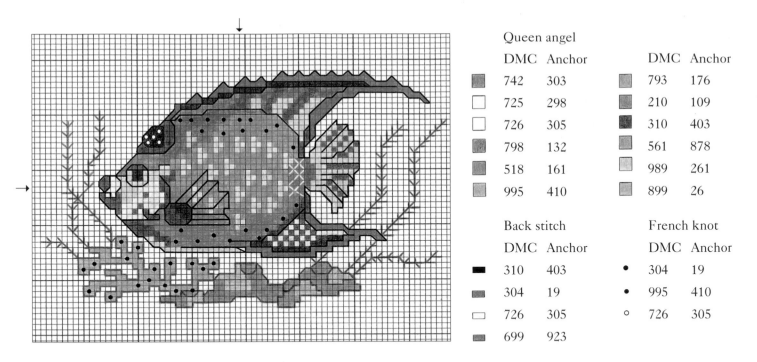

Queen angel

	DMC	Anchor		DMC	Anchor
▨	742	303	▨	793	176
☐	725	298	▨	210	109
☐	726	305	▨	310	403
▨	798	132	▨	561	878
▨	518	161	▨	989	261
▨	995	410	▨	899	26

Back stitch

	DMC	Anchor
▬	310	403
▬	304	19
☐	726	305
▬	699	923

French knot

	DMC	Anchor
●	304	19
●	995	410
○	726	305

THREADFIN

Work the outline of the fish and the fins and half the eye in back stitch, using one strand of DMC 310/Anchor 403, then complete the eye using one strand of DMC Blanc/Anchor 2. Sew the outline of the coral in back stitch, using one strand of DMC 304/Anchor 19, then use two strands to stitch the French knots. Stitch the seaweed in back stitch, using two strands of DMC 699/Anchor 923, and finally work round the rocks in back stitch, using one strand of this thread.

QUEEN ANGEL FISH

Work the following French knots: on the coral using two strands of DMC 304/Anchor 19, on the fish's head using two strands of DMC 995/Anchor 410 and on the body using two strands of DMC 726/Anchor 305. Sew the outline of the fish, fin and tail and also the gills and eyes in back stitch, using one strand of DMC 310/Anchor 403, then sew the outline of the coral in back stitch, using one strand of DMC 304/Anchor 19. Form the crosses at the base of the fish's tail with back stitch, using one strand of DMC 726/Anchor 305. Finally, outline the seaweed and rocks in back stitch, using two strands of DMC 699/Anchor 923 for the seaweed and one for the rocks.

MILLETSEED

Work the outline of the fish and the fins in back stitch, using one strand of DMC 310/Anchor 403. Outline the coral in back stitch, using one strand of DMC 304/Anchor 19, then outline the rocks in back stitch, using one strand of DMC 699/Anchor 923. Sew the anemones' tentacles in long stitch, using two strands of DMC 518/Anchor 1039, and sew the seaweed in back stitch, using two strands of DMC 699/Anchor 923. Work French knots on the coral using two strands of DMC 304/Anchor 19, and one for the eye using two strands of DMC 310/Anchor 403.

SADDLEBACK

Work the outline of the fish, the fin, eye and tail in back stitch, using one strand of DMC 310/Anchor 403. Outline the flat seaweed and the rocks in back stitch, using one strand of DMC 699/Anchor 923, then sew the feathery seaweed in back stitch, using two strands of this thread. Finally, sew French knots on the rocks using two strands of DMC 367/Anchor 210.

To treat the finished embroideries, see page 101.

To frame the pictures

Mount the pictures following the instructions on page 104 then frame them, or have them done professionally at a framers.

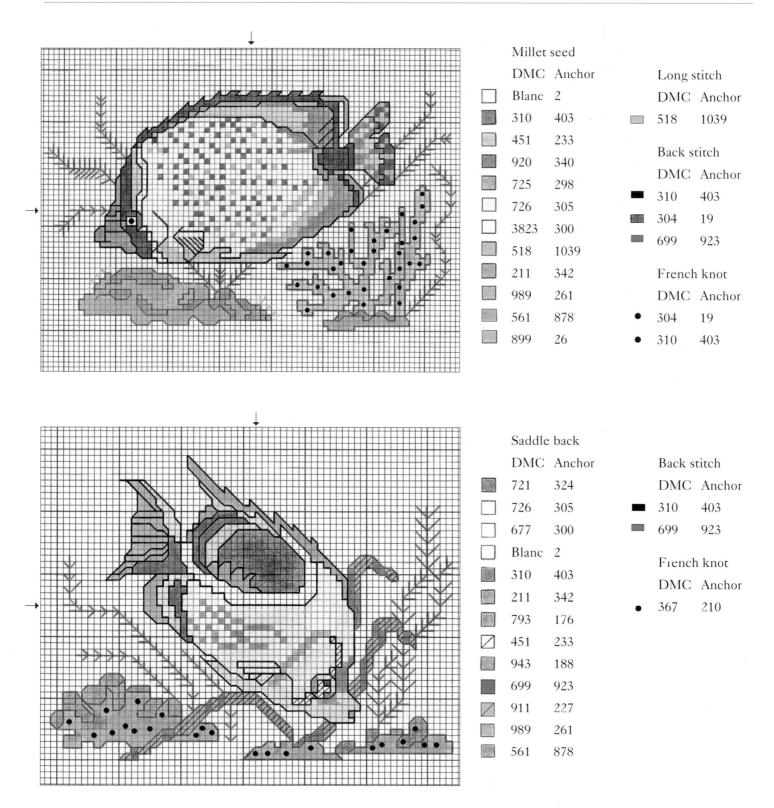

Millet seed

DMC	Anchor
Blanc	2
310	403
451	233
920	340
725	298
726	305
3823	300
518	1039
211	342
989	261
561	878
899	26

Long stitch

DMC	Anchor
518	1039

Back stitch

DMC	Anchor
310	403
304	19
699	923

French knot

DMC	Anchor
304	19
310	403

Saddle back

DMC	Anchor
721	324
726	305
677	300
Blanc	2
310	403
211	342
793	176
451	233
943	188
699	923
911	227
989	261
561	878

Back stitch

DMC	Anchor
310	403
699	923

French knot

DMC	Anchor
367	210

Pet Sampler

Samplers were made in the past by young women to practise their embroidery skills, and many are personal records of the stitcher's home, family and pets. When you have finished this sampler, you might feel confident enough to design one that incorporates your own pets.

Measurements
The finished embroidery size is 17.5 x 17.5cm (7 x 7in).

Materials
- Piece of 34 x 34cm (13⅜ x 13⅜in) beige 18-count Zweigart DMC Rustico Aida
- DMC or Anchor stranded embroidery cotton, one skein of each colour shown on the chart
- Tapestry needle size 24-26
- 20cm (8in) embroidery hoop
- Picture frame
- Acid-free mounting board
- Strong thread for stretching embroidery

To work the embroidery
Following the chart, start your embroidery from the centre of the markings you have placed on your Aida fabric (see page 101). Work the cross stitches with one strand of embroidery thread. When you have completed the cross stitching, sew the outline of the cat, dogs, bees and butterfly in back stitch, using one strand of DMC 310/Anchor 403. Use the same thread to sew the whiskers in long stitch and to work French knots for the dogs' and rabbits' eyes and for the antennae. Sew the grass in long stitch, using two strands of DMC 912/Anchor 209, then sew one long stitch and one back stitch on the turquoise ball of wool, using one strand of DMC 797/Anchor 139.

To treat the finished embroidery, see page 101.

To frame the embroidery
Mount the picture following the instructions on page 104 and then frame it, or have it done professionally at a framers.

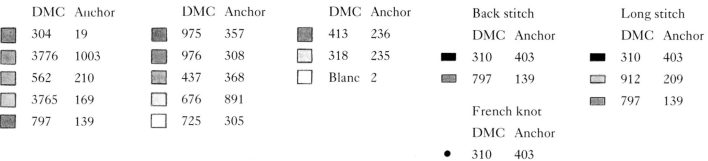

DMC	Anchor
304	19
3776	1003
562	210
3765	169
797	139

DMC	Anchor
975	357
976	308
437	368
676	891
725	305

DMC	Anchor
413	236
318	235
Blanc	2

Back stitch

DMC	Anchor
310	403
797	139

French knot

DMC	Anchor
310	403

Long stitch

DMC	Anchor
310	403
912	209
797	139

CLOTHING

A simple item of clothing can be transformed into something special by being embroidered with a design using waste canvas. Alternatively, you could try making your own items of clothing by incorporating embroidered Aida or Floba into the garment.

Baby Alligator Cap

American baby alligators are protected by their mothers for four years. When their strong markings begin to fade, they are able to fend for themselves.

Measurements

The finished embroidery size is 15.5 x 6cm
(6⅛ x 2⅜in).

Materials

- Piece of red 14-count Zweigart DMC Aida measuring 25.5 x 25.5cm (10 x 10in)
- DMC or Anchor stranded embroidery cotton, one skein of each colour shown on the chart
- Tapestry needle size 24-26
- 20cm (8in) embroidery hoop
- Commercial pattern for a peaked cap
- Piece each of red and green cotton, sufficient to make cap and lining, as directed by pattern, plus any other materials suggested
- Sewing machine
- Basic sewing kit

To work the embroidery

With a fabric marker, mark round the pattern piece for the top peak of the cap on the Aida. Following the chart, start your embroidery from the centre of the markings you have made on the Aida fabric (see page 101). Work the cross stitches with two strands of embroidery thread. When you have completed the cross stitching, sew the outline in back stitch using one strand of DMC 310/Anchor 403, then sew the teeth in ¼ cross stitch using two strands of DMC B5200/Anchor 1.

Treat the finished embroidery (see page 101), then make up the cap following the pattern.

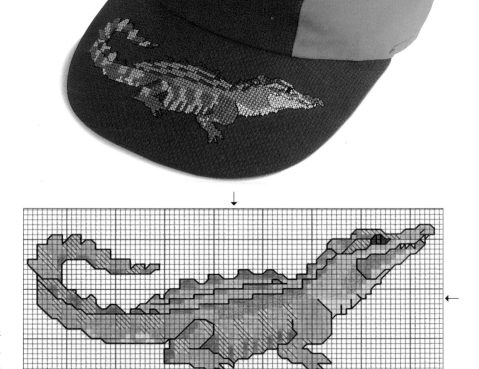

DMC	Anchor		DMC	Anchor		Back stitch	
						DMC	Anchor
B5200	1		703	225		310	403
310	403		731	281			
890	1044		644	830			
986	246		369	260			
701	227		725	298			

Bumble Bee Hat-Band

Bumble bees make their nests underground and feed their young on pollen and nectar.

Measurements

The finished embroidery size is 23 x 4cm (9 x 1½in).

Materials

- Strip of cream 16-count Zweigart DMC Aida measuring 129 x 5cm (51 x 2in)
- DMC or Anchor stranded embroidery cotton, one skein of each colour shown on the chart
- Tapestry needle size 24-26
- 15cm (6in) embroidery hoop
- Basic sewing kit

To work the embroidery

Following the chart, start your embroidery from the centre of the markings you have placed on your band of Aida fabric (see page 101). Work the cross stitches with two strands of embroidery thread. When you have completed the cross stitching, sew the outline of the bees and flowers in back stitch, using one strand of DMC 310/Anchor 403, and the bees' wing veins in back stitch, using one strand of DMC 3752/Anchor 975. Outline the flower stems in back stitch, using one strand of DMC 500/Anchor 683. Finally, sew French knots for the bees' eyes using one strand of DMC 310/Anchor 403, and French knots for the centre of the flowers using one strand of DMC 947/Anchor 332.

To treat the finished embroidery, see page 101.

To make up the hat-band

Cut the ends of the band at an angle, and turn under twice to hide the raw edges. Oversew by hand or top stitch by machine.

DMC	Anchor
632	936
676	891
3756	1037
744	301
742	303
367	210
704	255

Back stitch

DMC	Anchor
310	403
3752	975
500	683

French knot

DMC	Anchor
310	403
947	332

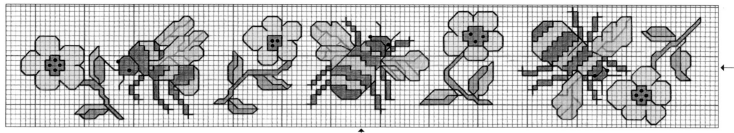

Pronghorn T-shirt

The pronghorn is a fast-running creature that grazes on the grasses, sagebrush and other plants of the North American prairies.

Measurements

The finished embroidery size is 8.3 x 5cm (3¼ x 2in).

Materials

- Piece of 14-count Zweigart DMC waste canvas measuring 15 x 10cm (6 x 4in)
- Piece of tear-away interfacing measuring 15 x 10cm (6 x 4in)
- DMC or Anchor stranded embroidery cotton, one skein of each colour shown on the chart
- Tapestry needle size 24-26
- 10cm (4in) or 15cm (6in) embroidery hoop
- Child's T-shirt
- Basic sewing kit

To work the embroidery

Mark where you want the embroidery to appear on the T-shirt, then mark out the central positioning lines on the waste canvas and match these to the marks on the T-shirt. See page 101 for directions on waste canvas embroidery. (See note below if T-shirt is very small.)

Following the chart, start your embroidery from the centre of the markings you have placed on your waste canvas (see page 101). Work the cross stitches with two strands of embroidery thread. When you have completed the cross stitching, sew the outline in back stitch, using one strand of DMC 310/Anchor 403. Work French knots for the eyes, using the same thread, and for the flowers, using one strand of DMC 743/Anchor 305. Finally, use one strand of DMC 988/ Anchor 257 to sew the grass in long stitch.

To treat the finished waste canvas embroidery, see page 101.

Note: If the T-shirt is very small, you may have to unpick one side seam to be able to fit the hoop onto the design. When the embroidery is complete, re-sew the side seam and hem as necessary, either by machine or by hand, and press.

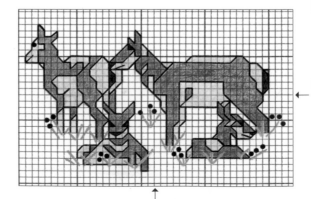

	DMC	Anchor
▨	632	936
▧	3072	397
☐	437	362
▨	988	257
■	310	403

Back stitch

	DMC	Anchor
▬	310	403

French knot

	DMC	Anchor
●	310	403
●	743	305

Hummingbird Blouse Collar

A humming bird hovers daintily, refreshing itself with some nectar before resuming its journey.

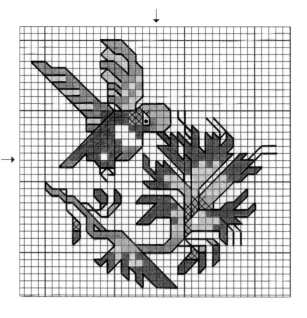

	DMC	Anchor
■	310	403
□	Blanc	2
■	3809	169
■	993	185
■	3814	188
■	919	341
■	3776	1048
⊠	722	323
■	350	11
□	744	305
■	3348	265
■	3345	268
⊠	470	266

Back stitch

	DMC	Anchor
■	310	403

French knot

	DMC	Anchor
●	310	403

Measurements
The finished embroidery size is 6.5 x 6.5cm (2½ x 2½in).

Materials
- Piece of Zweigart DMC waste canvas measuring 15 x 15cm (6 x 6in)
- Piece of tear-away fabric large enough to stretch over the embroidery hoop
- DMC or Anchor stranded embroidery cotton, one skein of each colour shown on the chart
- Tapestry needle size 24-26
- 15cm (6in) embroidery hoop
- Blouse or shirt with suitable collar
- Basic sewing kit

To work the embroidery
Decide where you would like the embroidery to be on the collar. Mark the central positioning lines on the waste canvas and match these to the lines on the collar. See page 101 for directions on waste canvas embroidery. (Note that you may have to pin and tack a piece of tear-away fabric behind the whole wing of the collar, large enough to place over an embroidery hoop, and then tack the waste canvas in position on top before starting to sew.)

Following the chart, start your embroidery from the centre of the markings you have placed on your waste canvas (see page 101). Work the cross stitches with two strands of embroidery thread. When you have completed the cross stitching, sew the outline in back stitch, using one strand of DMC 310/Anchor 403, then work a French knot for the eye, using the same thread.

To treat the finished waste canvas embroidery, see page 101.

Elephant Baby Bib

Elephants form small family herds of female and young elephants; when the young males are mature enough to leave their mothers, they join all-male herds. Enjoy cross stitching this little elephant bib for a new member of someone's family.

Measurements

The finished embroidery size is 12.5 x 5cm (5 x 2in).

Materials

- Piece of antique white 16-count Zweigart DMC Aida measuring 33 x 28cm (13 x 11in)
- DMC or Anchor stranded embroidery cotton, one skein of each colour shown on the chart
- Tapestry needle size 24–26
- 15cm (6in) embroidery hoop
- Template for bib (see page 108) and some card
- Piece of soft cotton fabric for the backing to the same size as the Aida

- 1.5m (5ft) of ready-made bias binding (or see page 104 if you want to make your own)
- Sewing machine
- Basic sewing kit

To work the embroidery

Trace the template on page 108 and transfer the outline onto the card. Cut it out. Place the bib pattern on the Aida, and draw round it. Cut out your bib shape. Position the design so that it rests on the line marked on the template, then start your embroidery from the centre of the chart. Work the cross stitches with two strands of embroidery thread. When you have completed

DMC	Anchor
646	8581
648	900
3072	397
310	403
Blanc	2

Long stitch

DMC	Anchor
Blanc	2
562	210

French knot

DMC	Anchor
310	403

Back stitch

DMC	Anchor
310	403

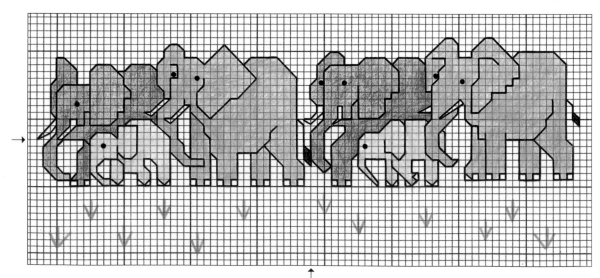

the cross stitching, sew the tusks in long stitch, using two strands of DMC Blanc/Anchor 2. Work French knots for the eyes, using one strand of DMC 310/Anchor 403, then use the same thread to outline the elephants in back stitch. Finally, sew the grass in long stitch, using two strands of DMC 562/Anchor 210

To treat the finished embroidery, see page 101.

To make up the bib

Use the card pattern to cut out a bib shape from the soft cotton fabric and place it to cover the wrong side of the embroidery; tack round the edges.

Cut two lengths of bias binding, one measuring 81.2cm (32in) and the other 66cm (26in); the longest piece is for edging round the bib and the other piece is for edging the top and forming the ties. Open out the longest piece of binding and pin and tack it all round the edge of the front of the bib (see page 104), right sides and raw edges together; then machine stitch along the crease of the bias strip. Press the sewn edge. Fold the bias over to the back of the bib to cover the raw edge, then pin, tack and over sew by hand to the backing.

Find the middle length of the shorter piece of bias and pin it, opened out, to the centre of the bib top (right sides and raw edges together). Pin, tack and machine stitch along the crease of the bias as before. Press and turn to the back of the bib, covering the raw edge. There will be a long piece extending at each side for the ties. Pin, tack and over sew by hand, from the begin-ning of one tie, along the back of the top and to the end of the other tie; knot the end of each tie to finish off the bib.

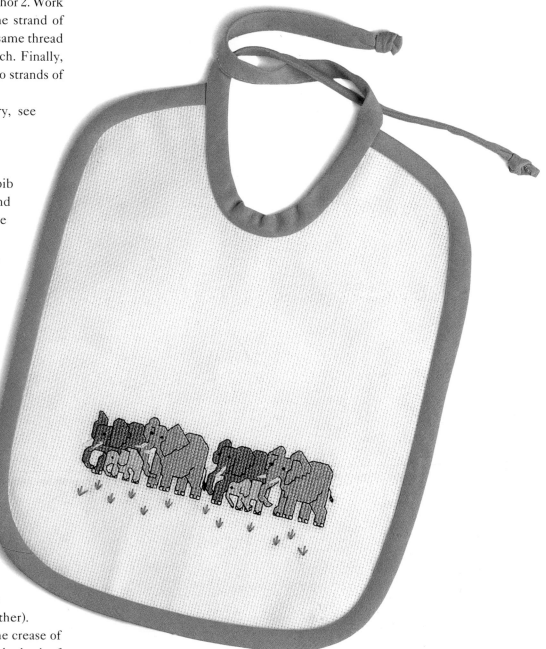

Chinstrap Penguin Scarf

Chinstrap penguins survive extreme cold with their dense, oily feathered coats and plenty of blubber.

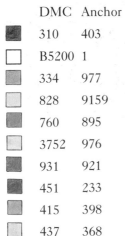

Measurements

The finished embroidery size is 8 x 5.5cm (3⅛ x 2⅛in).

Materials

- Piece of 14-count Zweigart DMC waste canvas measuring 10 x 12.5cm (4 x 5in)
- Piece of tear-away interfacing to the same size as the waste canvas
- DMC or Anchor stranded embroidery cotton, one skein of each colour shown on the chart
- Tapestry needle size 24-26
- 15cm (6in) embroidery hoop
- Fleecy scarf
- Basic sewing kit

To work the embroidery

Mark the centre of the scarf at one end with tacking thread, then measure up about 4cm (1½in) from the end and tack across the scarf at this point to mark where the embroidery will finish. On the waste canvas, mark out the central positional lines and where the embroidery will end, and match these marks to those on the scarf. See page 101 for directions on waste canvas embroidery.

Following the chart, start your embroidery from the centre of the markings you have placed on your waste canvas (see page 101). Work the cross stitches with two strands of embroidery thread. When you have completed the cross stitching, sew the outline of the penguin in back stitch, using one strand of DMC 310/Anchor 403, and the wing in back stitch, using one strand of DMC B5200/Anchor 1. Work French knots for the eyes using one strand of DMC 310/Anchor 403.

To treat the finished waste canvas embroidery, see page 101.

DMC	Anchor
310	403
B5200	1
334	977
828	9159
760	895
3752	976
931	921
451	233
415	398
437	368

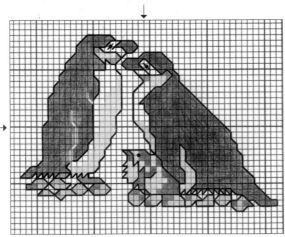

Kangaroo Dungarees

These kangaroos travel with great leaps and bounds across the vast grassy plains of Australia.

Measurements

The finished embroidery size is 5.5 x 10.5cm (2¼ x 4⅛in).

Materials

- Piece of Zweigart DMC waste canvas measuring 18 x 12.5cm (7 x 5in)
- Piece of tear-away interfacing to the same size as the waste canvas
- DMC or Anchor stranded embroidery cotton, one skein of each colour shown on the chart
- Tapestry needle size 24-26
- 15cm (6in) embroidery hoop
- Pair of plain-fronted dungarees
- Basic sewing kit

To work the embroidery

Centre the design on the dungaree bib front with tacking

thread, then follow the instructions for waste canvas embroidery on page 101.

Following the chart, start your embroidery from the centre of the markings you have placed on your waste fabric (see page 101). Work the cross stitches with two strands of embroidery thread. When you have completed the cross stitching, sew the outline of the kangaroos in back stitch, using one strand of DMC 310/Anchor 403, then use the same thread, twisted only once round the needle, to work French knots for the eyes. Sew the grass in long stitch, using two strands of DMC 700/Anchor 229.

To treat the finished waste canvas embroidery, see page 101.

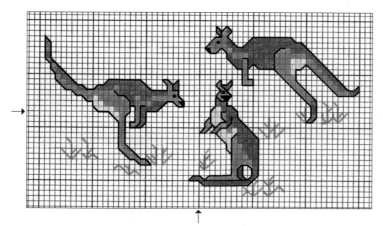

DMC	Anchor		
433	358		
782	308	Long stitch	
676	891	DMC	Anchor
310	403	700	229

Peacock Waistcoat

The peacock attracts the peahen by displaying his tail into a fan of many eyes and by shimmering his wings to show off his iridescent plumage.

Measurements

The finished embroidery sizes are 13 x 12.5cm (5⅛ x 4⅞in) for the waistcoat back and 6.5 x 6cm (2½ x 2⅜in) for both waistcoat fronts.

Materials

• Piece of 14-count Zweigart Floba, sufficient to make up an entire waistcoat from a commercial pattern. (Note that most patterns will assume that the back is to be made of satin lining, so take this into account when calculating how much Floba you will need.)
• Any other notions the pattern suggests

• DMC or Anchor stranded embroidery cotton, one skein of each colour shown on the chart
• Tapestry needle size 24-26
• 15cm (6in) embroidery hoop
• Sewing machine
• Basic sewing kit

To work the embroidery

Cut out the back and both fronts of the waistcoat and overlock or zig zag by machine all round the raw edges to stop them fraying. Work out the position in which you want to place each embroidered design, and tack in the central horizontal and vertical lines; place your hoop over the area to be sewn.

Following the chart, start your embroidery from the centre

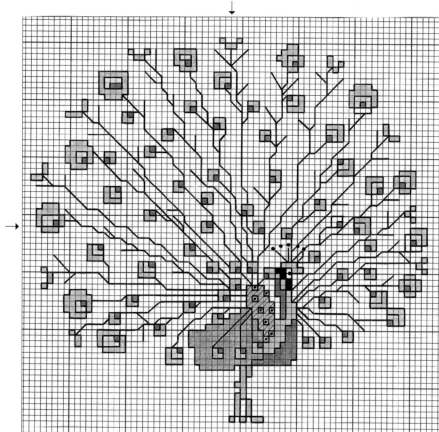

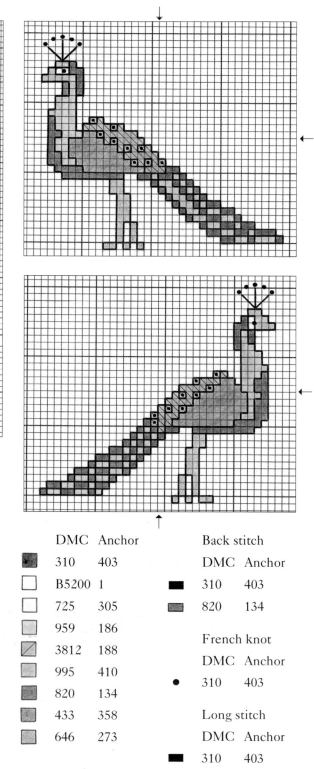

of the markings you have placed on your Floba fabric (see page 101). Work the cross stitches with two strands of embroidery thread. When you have completed the cross stitching, use one strand of DMC 310/Anchor 403 to outline the back peacock in back stitch, sew its crest in long stitch and work French knots for the crest, eye and back. Finally, sew the feather veins in back stitch, using two strands of DMC 820/Anchor 134, and outline the feather eyes in the same stitch and colour, but using just one strand. Repeat the outline stitching for the front peacocks using DMC 310/Anchor 403, then change to two strands for the crest and the French knots

To treat the finished embroidery, see page 101.

To make up the waistcoat
Follow the instructions on the commercial pattern to make up the waistcoat.

To treat the finished waste canvas embroidery, see page 101.

DMC	Anchor
310	403
B5200	1
725	305
959	186
3812	188
995	410
820	134
433	358
646	273

Back stitch

DMC	Anchor
310	403
820	134

French knot

DMC	Anchor
310	403

Long stitch

DMC	Anchor
310	403

Sleepy Owl Slippers

These handsome night birds make excellent companions for a pair of bedtime slippers.

Measurements

The finished embroidery size is 6 x 7cm
(2¼ x 2¾in).

Materials

- 2 pieces of 14-count Zweigart DMC waste canvas measuring 15 x 15cm (6 x 6in)
- Two pieces of tear-away interfacing to the same size as the waste canvas
- DMC or Anchor stranded embroidery cotton, one skein of each colour shown on the chart
- Tapestry needle size 24-26
- 15cm (6in) embroidery hoop
- Commercial slipper pattern
- Piece each of red and navy felt, measuring 46 x 46cm (18 x 18in)
- Piece of sheepskin or suede or a synthetic non-slip fibre for the sole, 28 x 28cm (11 x 11in), or longer if your foot is larger than a size 6
- Two pieces of red cord each 74cm (29in) long
- Leather hole puncher
- Large leather needle with a large eye
- Red double knitting wool
- Sewing machine
- Basic sewing kit

To work the embroidery

Mark round the slipper top pattern piece twice on the navy blue felt (reversing it once to make a pair). Do not cut out, but mark the desired position of the embroidery with tacking thread. Mark the central positioning lines on the waste canvas and match these to the lines on the felt. See page 101 for directions on waste canvas embroidery.

Following the chart, start your embroidery from the centre of the markings you have placed on your waste canvas (see page 101). Work the cross stitches with two strands of embroidery thread. When you have completed the cross stitching, sew round the eyes, beak and dark brown markings in back stitch, using one strand of DMC 310/Anchor 403.

To treat the finished waste canvas embroidery, see page 101.

To make up the slippers

Cut out the finished embroidered navy slipper tops, and mark and cut out two red felt linings to the same size. Place each navy piece on top of its lining and tack them together. Machine stitch with navy thread round the top edge twice to make a casing for the cord about 1cm (⅜in) wide.

Sew round the bottom edge of each slipper in navy thread, using running stitch to ease round the toe, then machine stitch up the back of each side of both heels, just to the start of the cord casing. Use a safety pin to thread each length of cord through one of the casings.

Mark round the sole pattern on the sheepskin twice, reversing the pattern once to make a pair. Punch holes round each sole with a leather puncher, about 1cm (⅜in) apart, and about 6mm (¼in) in from the edge of the sole.

Tack each sole onto a slipper, spreading the easing around the toe equally. Sew blanket stitch all round the edge of each slipper and sole, using two strands of knitting wool threaded through the leather needle. (The triangular point of the leather needle helps it to go through the two thicknesses of felt fabric.)

	DMC	Anchor
	310	403
	B5200	1
	898	381
	223	895
	742	303
	738	372
	435	369
	822	387
	744	305

Back stitch

	DMC	Anchor
	310	403

Chimpanzee Pocket Dress

Every evening, chimpanzees climb trees and there weave branches and leaves together to make comfortable nests.

Measurements

The finished embroidered size is 9 x 8cm (3½ x 3⅛in).

Materials

- Piece of white 14-count Zweigart DMC Aida measuring 20 x 20cm (8 x 8in)
- DMC or Anchor stranded embroidery cotton, one skein of each colour shown on the chart
- Tapestry needle size 24-26
- 15cm (6in) embroidery hoop
- Bought denim dress (child's)
- Pocket template (see page 110) and some card (for use with dress that has no pockets)
- Sewing machine
- Basic sewing kit

To work the embroidery

Following the chart, start your embroidery from the centre of the markings you have placed on your Aida fabric (see page 101). Work the cross stitches with two strands of embroidery thread. When you have completed the cross stitching, sew the outline of the monkey and tree, including the leaf veins, in back stitch, using one strand of DMC 310/Anchor 403, then use the same thread to work French knots for the eye and nostril.

Treat the finished embroidery (see page 101).

To make up the pocket

Carefully unpick one pocket from the dress and iron flat. Mark the central positioning lines on the pocket, then lay the embroidered Aida on top,

matching the lines. Cut the Aida into the same shape as the pocket. Place the pocket (which will form the lining) and the Aida right sides together, and machine along the top edge. Open out, and press the seam in the direction of the lining. Turn the pocket over and machine top stitch the lining close to the seam . The stitching will pass through the lining and both seam allowances. Fold the two sides of the pocket together so that it is inside out. Sew all round the sides and bottom, 1cm (⅜in) in, leaving a small gap halfway down one side. Trim the seam allowances, then pull the pocket through the gap to the right side. Press,

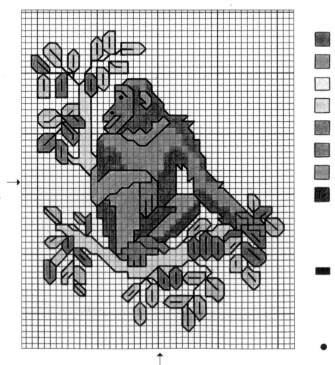

	DMC	Anchor
	3021	905
	433	358
	435	1046
	3348	265
	367	210
	3809	169
	223	895
	310	403

Back stitch

	DMC	Anchor
	310	403

French knot

	DMC	Anchor
●	310	403

then pin, tack and machine stitch in place.

If the dress has no pocket, use the template on page 110 and some card to make a pattern of the pocket shape; you will need to buy some cotton fabric to use for the pocket lining. Make up as above.

GIFTS

The practical and decorative gifts to make in this chapter, from the beautiful Valentine's heart to the present-stuffed advent calendar, will all make unusual and very welcome gifts.

Dolphin Cotton Wool Bag

These graceful mammals play gleefully in the water, their streamlined bodies leaping and diving through the waves.

Measurements

The finished embroidery size is 7 x 4cm (2¾ x 1⅝in).

Materials

- Piece of pale blue 14-count Zweigart DMC Aida measuring 30 x 30cm (11¾ x 11¾in)
- DMC or Anchor stranded embroidery cotton, one skein of each colour shown on the chart
- Tapestry needle size 24-26
- 15cm (6in) embroidery hoop
- White cotton lining fabric to the same size as the Aida
- Twisted cord (bought or homemade - see page 104), to match colour of dolphins, 81cm (32in) long
- Sewing machine
- Basic sewing kit

To work the embroidery

Mark the vertical central line of the Aida with tacking thread, then mark a horizontal line 9cm (3½in) up from the bottom of the fabric. The point where the two lines cross marks the centre of the design.

Following the chart, start your embroidery from the centre of the markings you have placed on your Aida fabric (see page 101). Work the cross stitches with two strands of embroidery thread. When you have completed the cross stitching, outline the dolphins in back stitch, using one strand of DMC 310/ Anchor 403, then use the same thread to work a French knot for each eye.

Treat the finished embroidery (see page 101), then make up the bag following instructions on page 105.

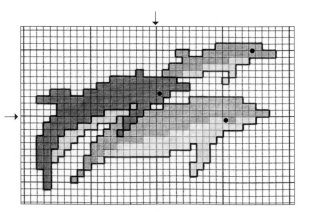

DMC	Anchor
3325	144
793	136
311	148

Back stitch

DMC	Anchor
310	403

French knot

DMC	Anchor
310	403

Magpie Jewellery Case

The magpie's love of bright things makes it an
appropriate choice for a jewellery case.

Measurements
The finished embroidery size is 10 x 6.5cm (4 x 2½in).

Materials
- Piece of blue-grey 14-count Zweigart DMC Aida measuring 51 x 28cm (20 x 11in)
- Additional piece of Aida (as above) for ties measuring 92 x 16cm (36 x 6in)
- DMC or Anchor stranded embroidery cotton, one skein of each colour shown on the chart
- Tapestry needle size 24-26
- 15cm (6in) embroidery hoop
- Piece of thin wadding, 48 x 19cm (19 x 7½in)
- Piece of lining fabric to size of wadding
- Sewing machine
- Basic sewing kit

To work the embroidery
Following the chart, start your embroidery from the centre of the markings you have placed on your Aida fabric (see page 101). Work the cross stitches with two strands of embroidery thread. When you have completed the cross stitching, sew the outline in back stitch, using one strand of DMC 310/Anchor 403, then continue with this cotton to work French knots for the eyes. Finally, sew the outline and veins of the leaves in back stitch, using one strand of DMC 319/Anchor 1044.

To treat the finished embroidery, see page 101.

To make up the jewellery case
Follow the instructions on page 106.

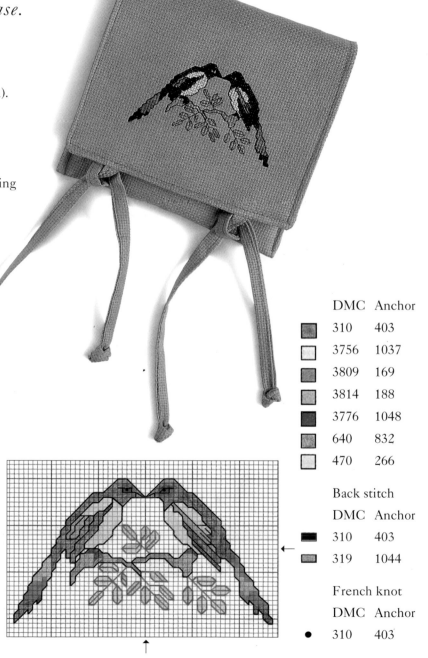

DMC	Anchor
310	403
3756	1037
3809	169
3814	188
3776	1048
640	832
470	266

Back stitch

DMC	Anchor
310	403
319	1044

French knot

DMC	Anchor
310	403

Love Birds Valentine Heart

These brightly coloured parrots from Africa are called love birds because of their loyalty and affection for each other.

Measurements

The finished embroidery size is 6 x 7cm (2⅜ x 2 ¾in).

Materials

- Piece of red 14-count Zweigart DMC Aida measuring 20 x 20cm (8 x 8in)
- DMC or Anchor stranded embroidery cotton, one skein of each colour shown on the chart
- Tapestry needle size 24-26
- 20cm (8in) embroidery hoop
- Heart template (see page 109) and some card
- 71cm (28in) of 12mm (½in) wide red satin ribbon
- 25cm (10in) of red cotton for frill and back of heart
- Wadding for stuffing
- Sewing machine
- Basic sewing kit

To work the embroidery

Following the chart, start your embroidery from the centre of the markings you have placed on your Aida fabric (see page 101). Work the cross stitches with two strands of embroidery thread. When you have completed the cross stitching, sew the outline of the birds in back stitch, using one strand of DMC 310/Anchor 403, then sew the divisions of the tail feathers, using one strand of DMC Blanc/Anchor 2.

To treat the finished embroidery, see page 101.

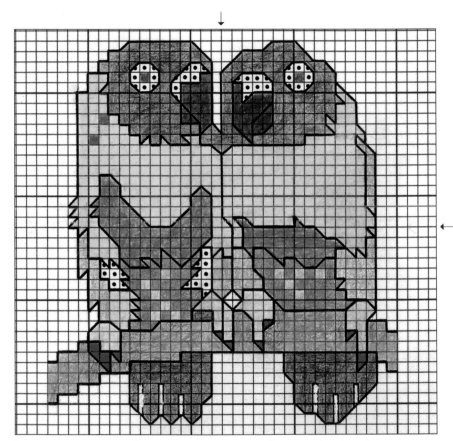

	DMC	Anchor
▓	310	403
▦	Blanc	2
░	453	231
▨	451	233
▨	700	229
░	703	238

	DMC	Anchor
░	742	303
▨	3340	330
▨	321	9046
▨	300	352

Back stitch

	DMC	Anchor
▬	310	403
▭	Blanc	2

To make up the heart

Trace the template on page 109 and transfer the outline onto the card. Cut it out and place it in the desired position over the embroidery. Mark round the pattern with a fabric marker and cut the heart out. Repeat for the back of the heart in red cotton fabric.

Cut the remaining red cotton fabric into bias strips 6cm wide x 91cm long (2½ x 36in) for the frill and join these up (see page 104) to make a long strip approximately twice the circumference of the heart. Press the frill in half lengthways, then sew two rows of gathering machine stitches up the length on the raw edges. Gather the frill to the required length.

Assemble the heart following the instructions on page 105, but push the wadding in through the gap before sewing it up by hand. To hang the heart, find the middle of the ribbon length and hand sew it to the top of the heart at the back.

Jay Scissor Case

During the autumn, jays collect acorns and bury them for extra food; many of the forgotten acorns grow into oak trees, so helping to replenish our woodlands.

Measurements

The finished embroidery size is 4.5 x 4cm (1¾ x 1½in).

Materials

- Piece of pale green 14-count Zweigart DMC Aida measuring 42 x 15cm (16½ x 6in)
- DMC or Anchor stranded embroidery cotton, one skein of each colour shown on the chart
- Tapestry needle size 24-26
- 10cm (4in) embroidery hoop
- Scissor case template (see pages 108-9) and some card
- Piece of lining fabric to the same size as the Aida
- 90cm (1yd) of twisted cord, either ready made or twisted yourself with two of the embroidery colours (see page 104)
- Sewing machine
- Basic sewing kit

To work the embroidery

Following the chart, start your embroidery from the centre of the markings you have placed on your Aida fabric (see page 101). Work the cross stitches with two strands of embroidery thread. When you have completed the cross stitching, sew the outline in back stitch, using one strand of DMC 310/Anchor 403. Use the same cotton to work a French knot for the eye.

To treat the finished embroidery, see page 101.

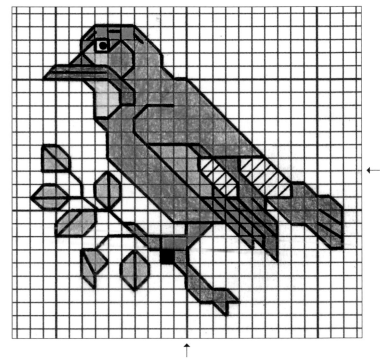

	DMC	Anchor
	316	1017
	995	410
	3042	870
	930	1036
	3743	869
	Blanc	2
	841	378
	704	255
	310	403

Back stitch

	DMC	Anchor
	310	403

French knot

	DMC	Anchor
	310	403

To make up the scissor case

Tack the embroidery marking lines out to the edge of the Aida. Trace the template on pages 108-9 and transfer the outline onto the card. Cut it out, and place it on top of the Aida, matching its central lines to those on the Aida. Pin it in place and tack round it. Mark where the fold lines of the case will be with tacking stitches. Mark round the card pattern with a fabric marker and cut out. Cut out the same shape from the lining fabric.

Assemble the layers of the scissor case following the instructions on page 105.

Fold the fabric into the scissor case shape, following the tacked fold lines, then pin, tack and top stitch down the sides of the case. Decorate with twisted cord, then hand sew a 30cm (12in) length of cord, folded in half, to the centre of the flap underside for the tie. Make a little buttonhole loop at the point where the edge of the flap lies, through which to tie the cord.

Octopus Pot Pourri Bag

When an octopus glides over rocks at the bottom of a lagoon, its colours change as it moves from shade to light.

Measurements

The finished embroidery size is
12 x 8cm (4¾ x 3⅛in).

Materials

- Piece of pale green 14-count Zweigart DMC Aida measuring 28 x 28cm (11 x 11in)
- DMC or Anchor stranded embroidery cotton, one skein of each colour shown on the chart
- Tapestry needle size 24-26
- 15cm (6in) embroidery hoop
- Piece of lining measuring 23.5 x 14cm (9¼ x 5½in)
- Piece of cord for tie, 76cm (30in) long
- Sewing machine
- Basic sewing kit

To work the embroidery

Draw a rectangle on the Aida measuring 23.5 x 14cm (9¼ x 5½in).

Centre the octopus motif so that the bottom of the design finishes 4cm (1½in) up from the bottom edge of the bag. Following the chart, start your embroidery from the centre of the markings you have made on the Aida (see page 101). Work the cross stitches with two strands of thread. When you have completed the cross stitching, sew the outline of the design (except for the starfish) in back stitch, using one strand of DMC 310/Anchor 403. Outline the starfish in back stitch, using one strand of DMC 825/Anchor 979.

Work French knots for the seaweed using one strand of DMC 470/Anchor 266 and for the starfish using one strand of DMC 996/Anchor 433.

Treat the finished embroidery (see page 101).

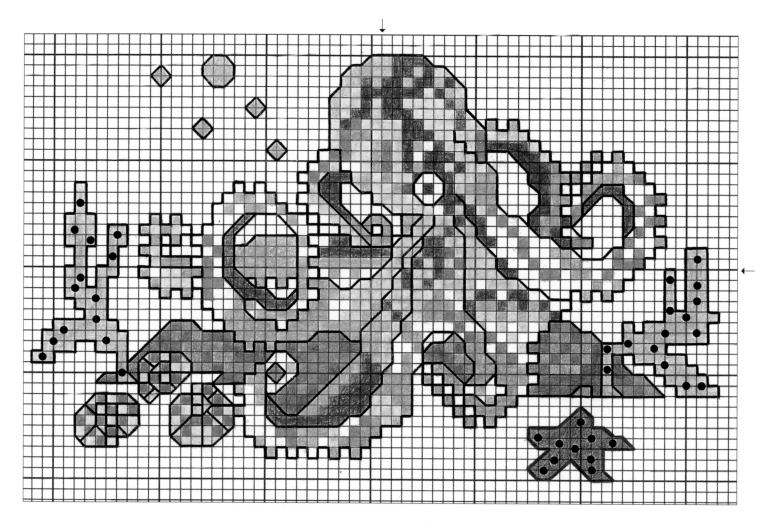

	DMC	Anchor		DMC	Anchor
☐	Blanc	2	▨	310	403
▨	827	159	▨	501	878
▨	996	433	▨	470	266
▨	825	979	☐	703	238
▨	642	392			
▨	420	375			
☐	676	891			
▨	3733	75			

Back stitch

	DMC	Anchor
▬	310	403
▬	825	979

French knot

	DMC	Anchor
•	470	266
•	996	433

To make up the bag

Follow the instructions on page 105 to make up the bag, but instead of sewing across the bottom of the Aida, gather it as follows, then turn the bag right side out and continue as directed.

To gather the bottom, sew two rows of gathering stitch at the bottom end of the Aida, either by machine or by hand. Pull the loose threads at either end to gather. (Because Aida is quite a stiff fabric, it will not gather to close up completely, so sew up the remaining hole with some machine stitching.)

When the bag is finished, fill with pot pourri.

Animal Advent Calendar

Each Christmas stocking, decorated with animals from all over the world, can be filled with a tiny gift.

Measurements

The finished embroidery sizes vary, but each fits well into the 10cm (4in) width of the foot of the Christmas stocking.

Materials

• Enough beige 18-count Zweigart DMC Floba for 24 stocking halves
• DMC or Anchor stranded embroidery cotton, one skein of each colour shown on the chart
• 15cm (6in) embroidery hoop
• Tapestry needle size 24-26
• Stocking template (see page 110)
• Enough red felt for 24 stocking halves
• 15cm (6in) of red cord or ribbon (x 24)
• Length of natural cord
• Sewing machine
• Basic sewing kit

To work the embroidery

Use the stocking template to mark out 24 stockings on the Floba fabric. Leave sufficient fabric all round to fit the pieces on the embroidery hoop, and cut out. Centre the design positions on the stockings and tack in with contrasting thread.

Following the chart, start your embroidery from the centre of the markings you have placed on your Floba fabric (see page 101). Work the cross stitches with one strand of embroidery thread. When you have completed the cross stitching, work French knots for the holly berries using one strand of DMC 304/Anchor 19 twisted three times round the needle. Stitch the holly leaf veins in back stitch, using one strand of DMC 319/Anchor 1044. Sew the outline (where indicated) in back stitch, using one strand of DMC 310/Anchor 403. Continue with this thread to sew any whiskers in long stitch and eyes in French knots, then sew the grass in long stitch, using two strands of DMC 910/Anchor 229.

To treat the finished embroidery, see page 101.

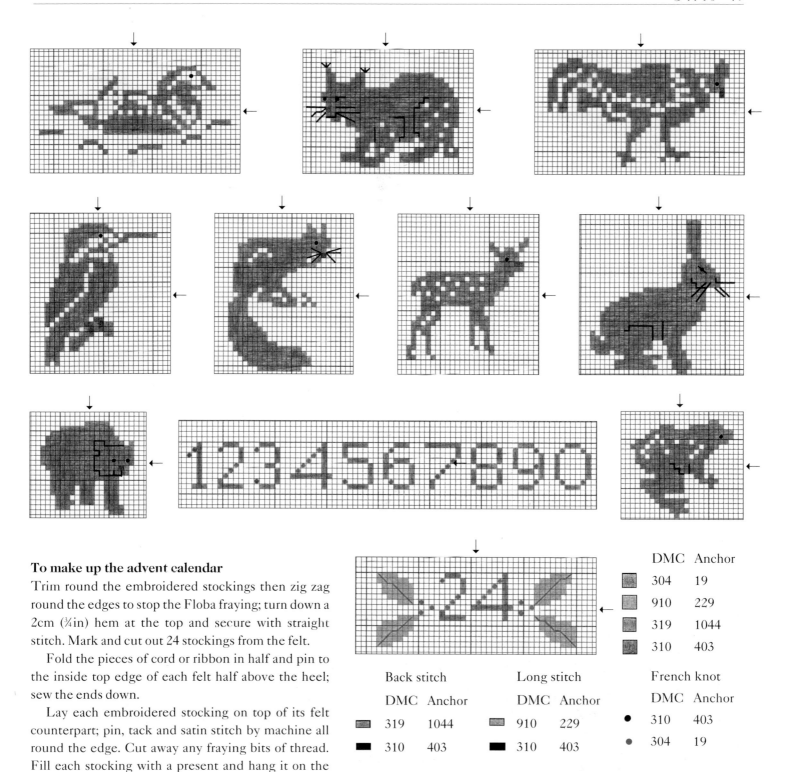

To make up the advent calendar

Trim round the embroidered stockings then zig zag round the edges to stop the Floba fraying; turn down a 2cm (¾in) hem at the top and secure with straight stitch. Mark and cut out 24 stockings from the felt.

Fold the pieces of cord or ribbon in half and pin to the inside top edge of each felt half above the heel; sew the ends down.

Lay each embroidered stocking on top of its felt counterpart; pin, tack and satin stitch by machine all round the edge. Cut away any fraying bits of thread. Fill each stocking with a present and hang it on the long length of natural cord.

For more charts, see over page (page 50).

DMC	Anchor
304	19
910	229
319	1044
310	403

Back stitch		Long stitch		French knot	
DMC	Anchor	DMC	Anchor	DMC	Anchor
319	1044	910	229	310	403
310	403	310	403	304	19

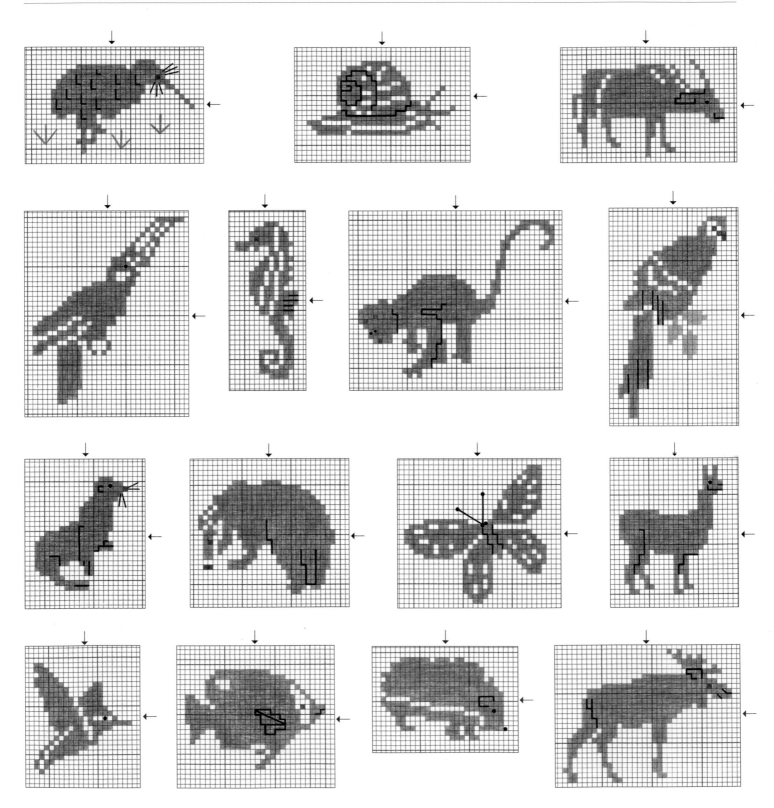

Red Squirrel Coaster

The red squirrel is rare now in England because of the successful invasion of its more aggressive cousin, the grey squirrel.

Measurements

The finished embroidery size is 7.5 x 7.5cm (3 x 3in).

Materials

- Piece of grey-blue 14-count Zweigart DMC 'Aida measuring 18 x 18cm (7 x 7in)
- DMC or Anchor stranded embroidery cotton, one skein of each colour shown on the chart
- Tapestry needle size 24-26
- 15cm (6in) embroidery hoop
- Clear plastic embroidery coaster
- Basic sewing kit

To work the embroidery

Following the chart, start your embroidery from the centre of the markings you have placed on your Aida fabric (see page 101). Work the cross stitches with two strands of embroidery thread. When you have completed the cross stitching, sew the outline in back stitch, using one strand of DMC 310/Anchor 403, then work the eyes in French knots, using the same thread twisted just once round the needle.

To treat the finished embroidery, see page 101.

To make up the coaster

Mark the circumference of the coaster with a fabric marker round the embroidered design, making sure the design is centred. Cut round the Aida, just inside the marked line. Pull the plastic

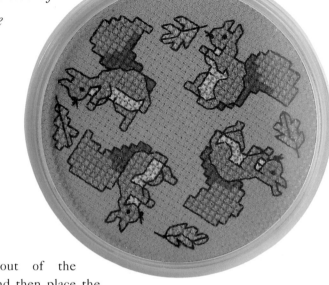

bottom out of the coaster and then place the embroidered design inside. Press the plastic bottom back into the coaster to secure the embroidered design.

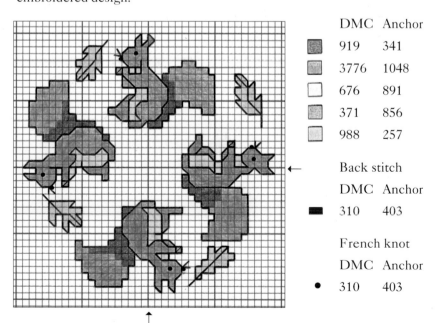

	DMC	Anchor
	919	341
	3776	1048
	676	891
	371	856
	988	257

Back stitch

	DMC	Anchor
	310	403

French knot

	DMC	Anchor
•	310	403

Fox Coffee Pot Cover

The male red fox is a good provider for his family and stays with his cubs until they are big enough to fend for themselves.

Measurements

The finished embroidery size is 13.5 x 6.5cm (5⅜ x 2⅝in).

Materials

- Piece of dark green 16-count Zweigart DMC Aida measuring 38 x 20cm (15 x 8in)
- DMC or Anchor stranded embroidery cotton, one skein of each colour shown on the chart
- Tapestry needle size 24-26
- 15cm (6in) embroidery hoop
- Lining and thin wadding to the same size as the Aida fabric
- 64cm (25¼in) of natural coloured cord
- Sewing machine
- Basic sewing kit

To work the embroidery

Following the chart, start your embroidery from the centre of the markings you have placed on your Aida fabric (see page 101). Work the cross stitches with two strands of embroidery thread. When you have completed the cross stitching, sew the outline of the foxes in back stitch, using one strand of DMC 310/Anchor 403. Using the same thread, sew the whiskers in long stitch and work the eyes in French knots. Finally, outline the rocks in back stitch, using two strands of DMC 562/Anchor 210, then use the same thread in long stitch to work the grass.

To treat the finished embroidery, see page 101.

To make up the coffee pot warmer

Measure your coffee pot from under the pouring lip to the bottom of the pot and round the circumference of its middle, then mark these dimensions on the embroidered Aida so that the embroidery is in the correct centred position. Cut out your piece of embroidered fabric to the size required, allowing 2cm (¾in) extra all round for seam allowances. Cut the cord into four equal lengths and place at the side seams of the cover, 4cm (1½in) in from the top and bottom edges. Knot the free end of each cord.

Cut out a piece each of the lining and wadding to the same size as the Aida. Assemble the layers of the warmer following the instructions on page 105, then tie the finished pot warmer round your coffee pot.

	DMC	Anchor
	310	403
	840	393
	300	357
	301	1049
	3376	1048
	738	366
	742	303
	367	217
	3052	261

Back stitch

	DMC	Anchor
	310	403
	562	210

Long stitch

	DMC	Anchor
	310	403
	562	210

French knot

	DMC	Anchor
●	310	403

Hare Glass Holder

Hares can be seen chasing each other in fields and having territorial boxing matches.

Measurements
The finished embroidery size is 11 x 6.5cm
(4⅜ x 2½in).

Materials
- Piece of dark green 16-count Zweigart DMC Aida measuring 30 x 15cm (12 x 6in)
- DMC or Anchor stranded embroidery cotton, one skein of each colour shown on the chart
- Tapestry needle size 24-26
- 15cm (6in) embroidery hoop
- Lining fabric to the same size as the Aida
- About 66cm (26in) of natural cotton cord

- Plastic canvas for base of glass holder
- Green felt to cover glass base
- Sewing machine
- Basic sewing kit

To work the embroidery
Following the chart, start your embroidery from the centre of the markings you have placed on your Aida fabric (see page 101). Work the cross stitches with two strands of embroidery thread. When you have completed the cross stitching, sew the outline in back stitch, using one strand of DMC 310/Anchor 403, then use the same thread

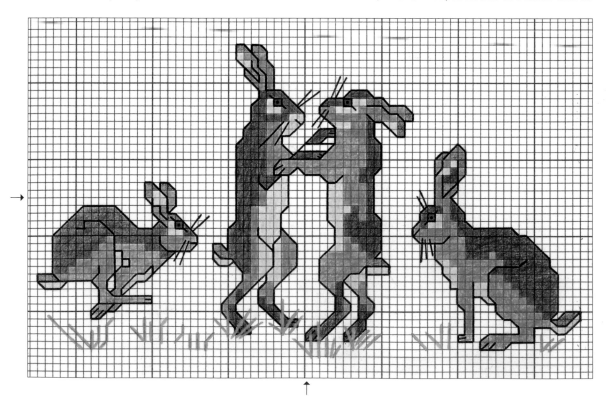

	DMC	Anchor
	844	1041
	632	357
	434	370
	676	891
	741	314

Back stitch

	DMC	Anchor
	310	403

Long stitch

	DMC	Anchor
	310	403
	562	230

French knot

	DMC	Anchor
	310	403

to sew the whiskers in long stitch and to work the eyes in French knots. Sew the grass in long stitch, using two strands of DMC 562/Anchor 230.

To treat the finished embroidery, see page 101.

To make up the glass holder

Measure the height to which the holder will come on your glass, then measure the width of your glass at that point. Add on 1cm (⅜in) for seam allowances all round, then cut the embroidered fabric to that size, centring the design so that it will lie opposite the back seam.

Fold the embroidered piece in half, right sides together, then sew up the centre back seam to make a cylinder; pull it through to the right side.

Fold the lining in half, right sides together, and sew up the centre back seam. Do not turn to the right side; instead, slip this over the main fabric, right sides together and matching centre seams, and machine stitch the two top edges together.

Turn the lining to the inside of the holder, making sure it does not show above the main fabric. Tuck the bottom edges up between the lining and the fabric, and neatly stitch in place.

Oversew the felt circle onto the plastic canvas circle, then oversew these to the base of the glass holder, with the felt piece showing at the base.

Decorate with cord at the top and bottom of the holder.

Badger Tea Cosy

The badger's strong front feet and claws are used for tunnelling out sets that are used for years by different generations of badgers.

Measurements

The finished embroidery size is 6 x 14.5cm (2½ x 5¾ in).

Materials

- Piece of grey-blue 14-count Zweigart DMC Aida large enough for one side of the tea cosy
- DMC or Anchor stranded embroidery cotton, one skein of each colour shown on the chart
- Tapestry needle size 24-26
- 15cm (6in) embroidery hoop
- Commercial pattern for a tea cosy
- Any other fabrics/materials required by the pattern
- Sewing maching
- Basic sewing kit

To work the embroidery

Place the relevant pattern piece on the Aida fabric, and mark its position with a fabric marker. Following the chart, start your embroidery from the centre of the markings you have placed on your Aida fabric (see page 101). Work the cross stitches with two strands of embroidery thread. When you have completed the cross stitching, sew the outline of the badger and grass in back stitch, using one strand of DMC 310/Anchor 403, then use the same thread to stitch the badger's whiskers in long stitch and to work a French knot for the eye. Finally, sew the small blades of brass in long stitch, using two strands of DMC 986/Anchor 246.

To treat the finished embroidery, see page 101.

To make up the tea cosy

Cut out the rest of the pattern pieces from your chosen fabrics and make the tea cosy following the pattern instructions.

	DMC	Anchor
■	310	403
▨	413	236
☐	414	233
◹	648	398
⊠	370	856
▨	642	392
▨	435	1046
▨	986	246
☐	703	238
☐	Blanc	2

Back stitch

	DMC	Anchor
▬	310	403

Long stitch

	DMC	Anchor
▬	310	403
▭	986	246

French knot

	DMC	Anchor
•	310	403

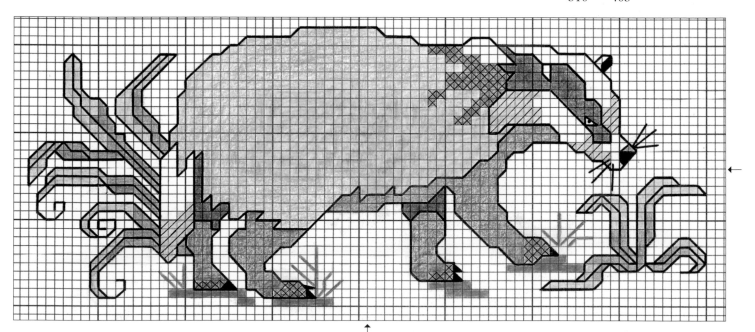

Harvest Mouse Napkin Tie

Harvest mice live in cereal fields and make their nests out of rolled-up balls of dried grass.

Measurements
The finished embroidery size is 9.5 x 2.5cm (3¾ x 1in).

Materials
- Piece of cream 16-count Zweigart DMC Aida measuring 45 x 12.5cm (17¾ x 5in)
- DMC or Anchor stranded embroidery cotton, one skein of each colour shown on the chart
- Tapestry needle size 24-26
- 10cm (4in) embroidery hoop
- Piece of lining fabric to the same size as the Aida
- Sewing machine
- Basic sewing kit

To work the embroidery
Following the chart, start your embroidery from the centre of the markings you have placed on your Aida fabric (see page 101). Work the cross stitches with two strands of embroidery thread. When you have completed the cross stitching, sew the outline of the mouse in back stitch, using one strand of DMC 433/Anchor 358. Use the same thread to stitch the whiskers in long stitch and to work a French knot for the eye. Finally, sew the corn stems in back stitch, using two strands of DMC 782/Anchor 308.

To treat finished embroidery, see page 101.

To make up the napkin tie
Measure 5cm (2in) in from each short end of the Aida, and mark this distance on both long edges. From each of these marks, draw lines out to meet in the middle of each short fabric edge, thus making a point at each end of the tie. Cut out a piece of lining to the same size. Assemble the napkin tie layers following the instructions on page 105.

DMC	Anchor
433	358
782	308
3776	1048
437	891
744	301
3779	868
746	386

Back stitch

DMC	Anchor
433	358
782	308

Long stitch

DMC	Anchor
433	358

French knot

DMC	Anchor
433	358

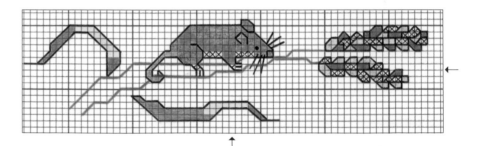

Swan Hand Towel

A mute swan will retract his head and open out his wings when displaying himself and when he wants to be threatening.

Measurements
The finished embroidery size is 11.5 x 5cm (4½ x 2in).

Materials
- Piece of pure white 14-count Zweigart DMC Aida measuring 25.5 x 25.5cm (10 x 10in)
- DMC or Anchor stranded embroidery cotton, one skein of each colour shown on the chart
- Tapestry needle size 24-26
- 15cm (6in) embroidery hoop
- Plain white hand towel
- Piece of thin wadding, 12.5 x 12.5cm (5 x 5in) (optional)
- Sewing machine
- Basic sewing kit

To work the embroidery
Following the chart, start your embroidery from the centre of the markings you have made on the Aida (see page 101). Work the cross stitches with two strands of embroidery thread. When you have completed the cross stitching, sew the outline of the swan in back stitch, using one strand of DMC 310/Anchor 403. Use the same thread to work a French knot for the swan's eye.

To treat the finished embroidery, see page 101.

To make up the towel
Cut the embroidered fabric to 14 x 14cm (5½ x 5½in), making sure the design is central to the cut fabric. If you want to give the appliquéd swan a slightly quilted look, add a piece of wadding between it and the towel. Cut the wadding to 3mm (⅛in) smaller than the 14cm (5½in) square. Position the embroidered square on the towel, placing the wadding (if used) between it and the towel. Turn under a 1.5cm (⅜in) hem all round the square and tack into position. Machine top stitch the design onto the towel.

	DMC	Anchor
▱	B5200	1
▪	310	403
▪	350	11
▪	800	9159
▪	341	939
▪	762	234
▫	3823	386

Back stitch

	DMC	Anchor
▬	310	403

French knot

	DMC	Anchor
●	310	403

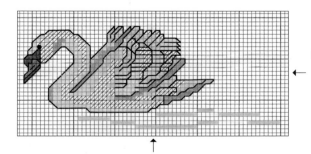

SOFT FURNISHINGS

*To ring the changes to your soft furnishings, embroider some wild animals
from exotic regions of the world. A leopard languishing on his branch on
the curtain tie-back or a lion gazing haughtily into the heat-hazed distance
on the bolster cushion should transport you to sunnier climes.*

Armadillo String Holder

Armadillos are burrowing animals that feed on snakes and insects. Put a ball of string inside this one and pull the string through the hole in place of his tail.

Measurements

The finished embroidery size is 9 x 5.5cm (3½ x 2¼in).

Materials

- Piece of antique white 16-count Zweigart DMC Aida measuring 30 x 18cm (12 x 7in)
- DMC or Anchor stranded embroidery cotton, one skein of each colour shown on the chart
- Tapestry needle size 24-26
- 15cm (6in) embroidery hoop
- Piece of lining fabric to the same size as the Aida
- Cotton cord for handles, 36cm (14in) long, cut in two
- Sewing machine
- Basic sewing kit

To work the embroidery

Centre the armadillo design on the piece of Aida, so that the head is facing one of the shorter sides. Following the chart, start your embroidery from the centre of the markings you have placed on the Aida fabric (see page 101). Work the cross stitches with two strands of thread. When you have completed the cross stitching, sew the outline in back stitch, using one strand of DMC 310/Anchor 403, then sew the grass in long stitch, using two strands of DMC 470/Anchor 266.

To treat the finished embroidery, see page 101.

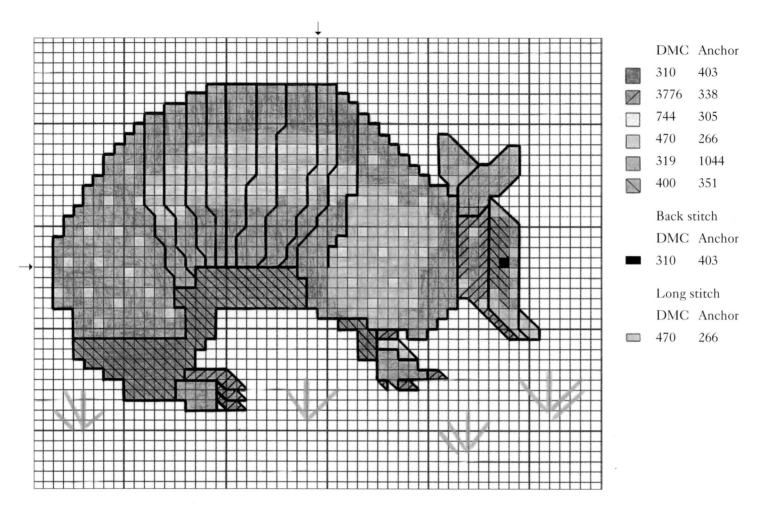

DMC	Anchor
310	403
3776	338
744	305
470	266
319	1044
400	351

Back stitch

DMC	Anchor
310	403

Long stitch

DMC	Anchor
470	266

To make up the bag

Snip a hole underneath the tail area of the armadillo, about two to three squares away from the embroidery. Oversew round the hole to stop the threads from fraying, then buttonhole stitch all round the edge of the hole for extra strength.

Fold the Aida right sides together and sew up the centre back seam. Adjust the tube so that the seam lies at the centre of the back, then sew across the bottom of the bag. Turn right side out. Position one of the handles on the outside of the bag so that it straddles the centre back seam and its ends are about 7cm (2 ¾in) apart. At this stage, the handle loop should be hanging down towards the bottom of the bag, with its ends aligned with the top of the bag. Machine stitch across the two raw ends of the handle to secure it. Repeat this process for the other handle on the opposite side of the Aida.

Attach the lining following the instructions on page 106 (note that the handles will be sandwiched between the lining and the bag). Mark the position of the string hole through onto the lining with a pin. Turn the whole bag inside out and cut a small hole into the marked position on the lining. Turn in the raw edges of the hole, tack it to the hole on the inside of the bag, then oversew round this double-layer hole by hand. Press the lining gently to neaten and turn the bag the right way round again. Press again.

Eider Duck Pillowcase

The eider duck lives near the sea and nests among boulders and stones, padding its nest with its famous downy feathers.

Measurements
The finished embroidery size is 20 x 5cm (8 x 2in).

Materials
- Piece of 14-count Zweigart DMC waste canvas measuring 30 x 15cm (12 x 6in)
- Piece of tear-away interfacing to the same size as the waste canvas
- DMC or Anchor stranded embroidery cotton, one skein of each colour shown on the chart
- Tapestry needle size 24-26
- 10cm (4in) embroidery hoop
- White cotton pillowcase
- Basic sewing kit

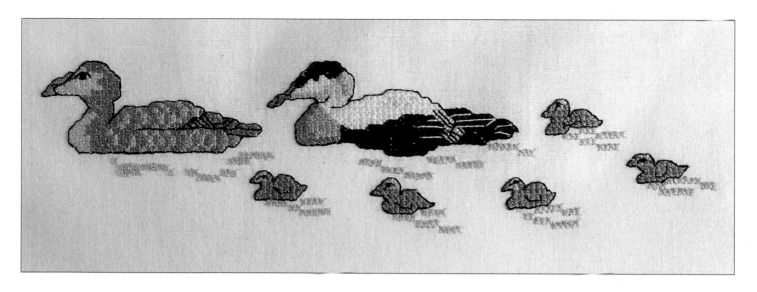

To work the embroidery

Centre the duck design in the chosen position on the pillowcase, then mark the central positioning lines on the waste canvas and match these to the lines on the pillowcase. See page 101 for directions on waste canvas embroidery. (If you decide to embroider on the edge, check that the pillowcase flap is not in the way of the embroidery position. If it is, you may have to unpick the sides of the pillowcase at this point to pull the flap back in order to have room to work the design.) Following the chart, start your embroidery from the centre of the markings you have made on your waste canvas (see page 101). Work the cross stitches with two strands of thread. When you have completed the cross stitching, sew the outline and the detailing of the duck, drake and ducklings in back stitch, using one strand of DMC 310/Anchor 403. Use the same thread to work French knots for all the birds' eyes, twisting the thread just once round the needle. Finally, sew the drake's tail in long stitch, using one strand of DMC 3823/Anchor 386.

To treat the finished waste canvas embroidery, see page 101.

If you had to unpick the flap, then re-sew it into position by hand or machine when the embroidery is finished.

	DMC	Anchor
■	310	403
■	402	1047
☐	3823	386
■	676	891
■	369	260
■	3052	859
■	3776	1048
■	840	898
■	644	391
■	3752	975

Back stitch

	DMC	Anchor
▬	310	403

Long stitch

	DMC	Anchor
☐	3823	386

French knot

	DMC	Anchor
●	310	403

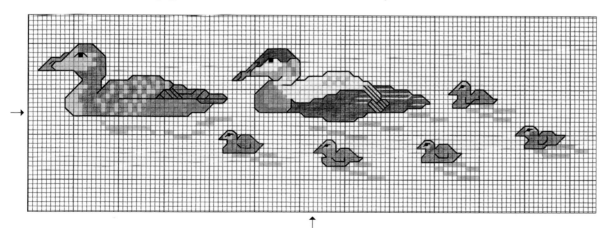

Lion Bolster Cushion

During the evening, the proud lion will utter a loud roar that can be heard from far away. This is to let other males know not to encroach on his territory. His fierce stance, with raised tail, shows that he is more than ready to protect his land, should any animal come too near.

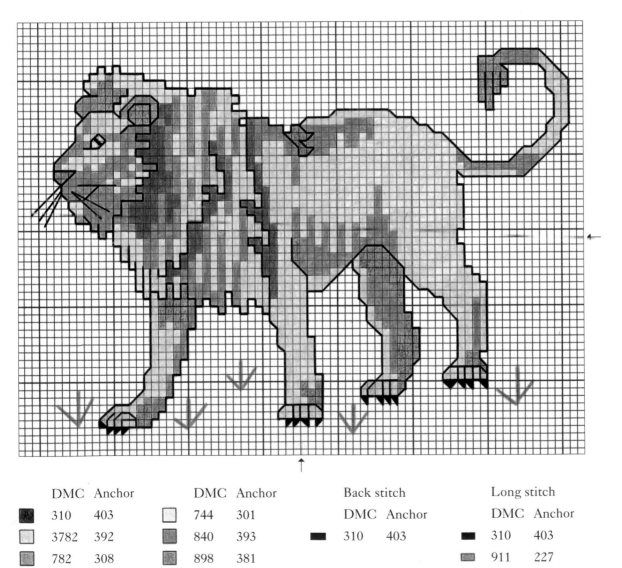

	DMC	Anchor		DMC	Anchor	Back stitch			Long stitch	
■	310	403	□	744	301	DMC	Anchor		DMC	Anchor
▨	3782	392	▨	840	393	■ 310	403		■ 310	403
▨	782	308	▨	898	381				▨ 911	227

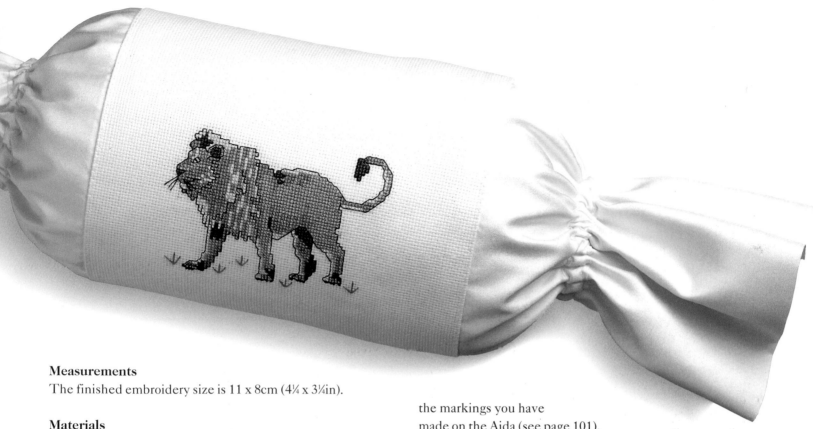

Measurements

The finished embroidery size is 11 x 8cm (4¼ x 3¼in).

Materials

- Piece of antique white 16-count Zweigart DMC Aida measuring 21cm (8¼in) wide and long enough to fit round the circumference of your bolster cushion pad
- DMC or Anchor stranded embroidery cotton, one skein of each colour shown on the chart
- Tapestry needle size 24-26
- 20cm (8in) embroidery hoop
- Bolster cushion pad
- Commercial pattern for a bolster cushion cover
- Fabric for cushion cover as suggested by pattern, plus any other materials needed
- *or* Ready-made bolster cushion cover
- Sewing machine
- Basic sewing kit

To work the embroidery

Centre the lion in the middle of the length of the Aida. Following the chart, start your embroidery from the centre of the markings you have made on the Aida (see page 101). Work the cross stitches with two strands of embroidery thread. When you have completed the cross stitching, sew the outline of the lion in back stitch, using one strand of DMC 310/Anchor 403, then use the same thread to sew the whiskers in long stitch. Finally, sew the clumps of grass in long stitch using DMC 911/Anchor 227.

To treat the finished embroidery, see page 101.

To make up the bolster cover

Cut out the fabric following the pattern instructions. Position the embroidered strip of Aida so that it lies round the middle circumference of the bolster cushion. Turn under the raw edges of the embroidered fabric, then pin, tack and top stitch it to the bolster fabric. Sew up the cover as instructed.

If you have chosen to use a ready-made cushion cover, you may have to unpick the seams and open out the fabric in order to appliqué the embroidered strip into position with ease.

Zebra Stool Cushion

Zebras are striking looking animals with very definite markings that vary from group to group. They show their sociable nature and family ties by grooming each other.

Measurements

The finished embroidery size is 11 x 7.5cm (4¼ x 3in).

Materials

- Piece of white 14-count Zweigart DMC Aida measuring approx. 5cm (2in) larger than the diameter of your stool pattern
- DMC or Anchor stranded embroidery cotton, one skein of each colour shown on the chart
- Tapestry needle size 24-26
- 15cm (6in) embroidery hoop
- Sheet of paper for pattern
- Wadding and lining fabric to the same size as the Aida
- Extra lining fabric to make ties (see making-up instructions opposite for measurements)
- Length of cord to trim round stool cover
- Sewing machine
- Basic sewing kit

To work the embroidery

Make a pattern of your stool with paper and add on a 1cm (⅜in) seam allowance all round. Pin the pattern to the Aida fabric and mark round it with

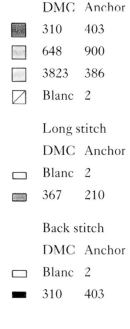

DMC	Anchor
310	403
648	900
3823	386
Blanc	2

Long stitch

DMC	Anchor
Blanc	2
367	210

Back stitch

DMC	Anchor
Blanc	2
310	403

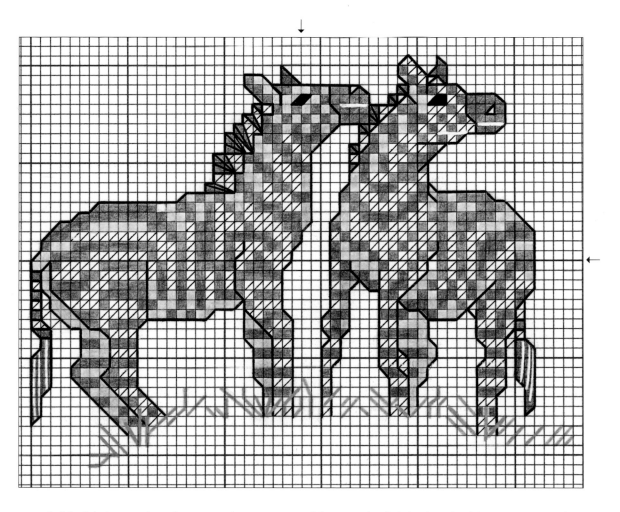

a washable fabric pen, but do not cut it out yet. Decide where you want your embroidery to go and draw the positioning lines. Following the chart, start your embroidery from the centre of the markings you have placed on your Aida fabric (see page 101). Work the cross stitches with two strands of embroidery thread. When you have completed the cross stitching, sew the outline of the zebras in back stitch, using one strand of DMC 310/Anchor 403. Sew the tails in long stitch, using one strand of DMC Blanc/Anchor 2 then use the same thread to back stitch round the nostrils and mouths. Finally, sew the clumps of grass in long stitch, using two strands of DMC 367/210 Anchor.

To treat the finished embroidery, see page 101.

To make up the stool cushion
Cut out the embroidered Aida, then cut out this same shape from the wadding and lining. Cut out four equal strips of fabric, 4cm (1½in) wide and long enough to tie the cover round a stool leg. Turn in both raw edges down the length of each tie, then pin, tack and top stitch down to secure. Assemble the cover layers following the instructions on page 105, placing the ties in pairs at the edge of the cover, one on top of the other, so that they may be tied round two opposite stool legs.

Add the finishing touch by hand sewing a cord trim all round the cushion.

Flying Fish Tissue Box Cover

A flying fish gathers speed with its tail under water then rises up, spreading its wings in the air, and glides as far as it can to avoid its predators.

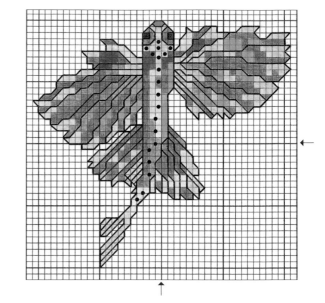

Measurements

The finished embroidery size is
7 x 7cm (2¾ x 2¾in).

Materials

- 2 pieces of 14-count Zweigart DMC waste canvas each measuring 12.5 x 12.5cm (5 x 5in)
- 2 pieces of tear-away interfacing, as above
- DMC or Anchor stranded embroidery cotton, one skein of each colour shown on the chart
- Tapestry needle size 24-26
- 15cm (6in) embroidery hoop
- Commercial tissue box cover pattern
- Any other fabrics/materials required by the pattern
- Sewing machine
- Basic sewing kit

To work the embroidery

Mark out the pattern piece to be embroidered on the fabric of your choice. Cut it out roughly, but not to the markings. Mark the central positioning lines for both flying fish motifs on the waste canvas and match these to both sets of lines on the fabric.

See page 101 for directions on waste canvas embroidery.

Following the chart, start embroidering the first motif from the centre of these markings on your waste canvas (see page 101). Work the cross stitches with two strands of embroidery thread. When you have completed the cross stitching, use one strand of DMC 310/Anchor 403 to outline the fish and to work the French knots where marked. Repeat for the other flying fish motif.

To treat the finished waste canvas embroidery, see page 101.

To make up the tissue box cover

Cut out the rest of the pattern pieces and sew up, following the pattern instructions.

DMC	Anchor
632	936
742	303
745	301
3776	1048
827	159
943	188
996	433
310	403

Back stitch

DMC	Anchor
310	403

French knot

DMC	Anchor
310	403

Seahorse Table Mat

Some types of seahorse look just like pieces of seaweed and so are easily camouflaged.

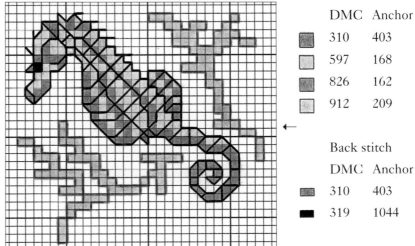

Measurements
The finished embroidery size is 6 x 5.5cm (2½ x 2¼in).

Materials
- Piece of pale green 14-count Zweigart DMC Aida measuring 25.5 x 25.5cm (10 x 10in)
- DMC or Anchor stranded embroidery cotton, one skein of each colour shown on the chart
- Tapestry needle size 24-26
- 15cm (6in) embroidery hoop
- Sewing machine
- Basic sewing kit

To work the embroidery
Following the chart, start your embroidery from the centre of the markings you have placed on your Aida fabric (see page 101). Work the cross stitches with two strands of embroidery thread. When you have completed the cross stitching, sew the seahorse outline in back stitch, using one strand of DMC 310/Anchor 403, then sew round the seaweed in back stitch, using one strand of DMC 319/Anchor 1044.

To treat the finished embroidery, see page 101.

To make up the mat
Mark and cut out the mat in the size you want, then machine stitch round the Aida, about 2cm (¾in) in from the edge. Fray the edges of the finished mat.

DMC	Anchor
310	403
597	168
826	162
912	209

Back stitch

DMC	Anchor
310	403
319	1044

Antelope Door Stop

*The greater kudu –
a type of antelope –
inhabits the Savanna
grasslands and
survives in parts of
Africa where other
antelope are scarce.
It feeds only at night
and rests in the day.*

Measurements
The finished embroidery size is 10.5 x 10.5cm (4¼ x 4¼in).

Materials
- Piece of royal blue 14-count Zweigart DMC Aida measuring 42 x 23cm (16½ x 9in)
- DMC or Anchor stranded embroidery cotton, one skein of each colour shown on the chart
- Tapestry needle size 24-26
- 15cm (6in) embroidery hoop
- Piece of calico measuring 36 x 23cm (14 x 9in)
- 36cm (14in) length of 1cm (⅜in) wide touch and close tape
- Sand or bean bag stuffing sufficient to fill the door stop
- Sewing machine
- Basic sewing kit

To work the embroidery
Fold the Aida in half widthways to form two 21 x 23cm (8¼ x 9in) shapes. Mark the fold line with tacking thread, then unfold. Centre the design position so that the head is near the

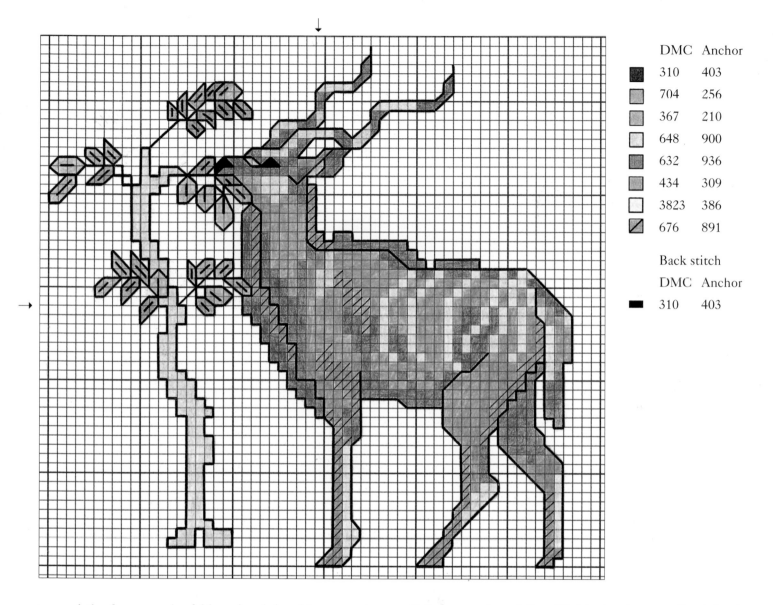

DMC	Anchor
310	403
704	256
367	210
648	900
632	936
434	309
3823	386
676	891

Back stitch

DMC	Anchor
310	403

top and the feet near the fold, and tack in with contrasting thread. Following the chart, start your embroidery from the centre of the markings on the Aida fabric (see page 101). Work the cross stitches with two strands of thread. When you have completed the cross stitching, sew the outline in back stitch, using one strand of DMC 310/Anchor 403.

To treat the finished embroidery, see page 101.

To make up the door stop

Fold the calico in half as for the Aida. Pin, tack and sew round all three raw edges, 1.5cm (⅝in) in, leaving a small gap for the stuffing. Turn the lining through to the right side and pour in the sand or beans. Oversew the gap closed by hand.

Fold over 2.5cm (1in) to the inside at the top and bottom of the Aida. Cut the strip of touch and close tape in half and lay one piece on each hem; stitch into place along the top and bottom of the tape. Fold the Aida in half at the fold line, right sides together. Pin, tack and sew up the side seams of the bag. Place the full lining bag inside the embroidered bag and press the top edges together to close the bag.

Leopard Curtain Tie-Back

The leopard hunts by night and spends most of the day lazing on the branch of a tree.

Measurements

The finished embroidery size is 9 x 17.5cm
(3½ x 7in).

Materials

• Piece of royal blue 14-count Zweigart DMC
  Aida measuring 66 x 15cm (26 x 6in)
• DMC or Anchor stranded embroidery cotton,
  one skein of each colour shown on the chart
• Tapestry needle size 24-26
• 20cm (8in) embroidery hoop
• Tie-back template (see pages 108-9) and some
  card
• Piece of lining fabric to the same size as the
  Aida
• Two pieces of iron-on interfacing to the same
  size as the Aida
• 2 brass rings or some cotton cord for loops
• Sewing machine
• Basic sewing kit

To work the embroidery

Trace the template on pages 108-9 and transfer
the outline onto the card. Cut it out, then mark
round the pattern on the Aida. The leopard
design should be positioned slightly to the right
or the left of the tie-back centre, so that it shows
when it is holding a curtain back. Reverse the
template, if necessary, to achieve the position you
want. Following the chart, start your embroidery
from the centre of the markings you have placed

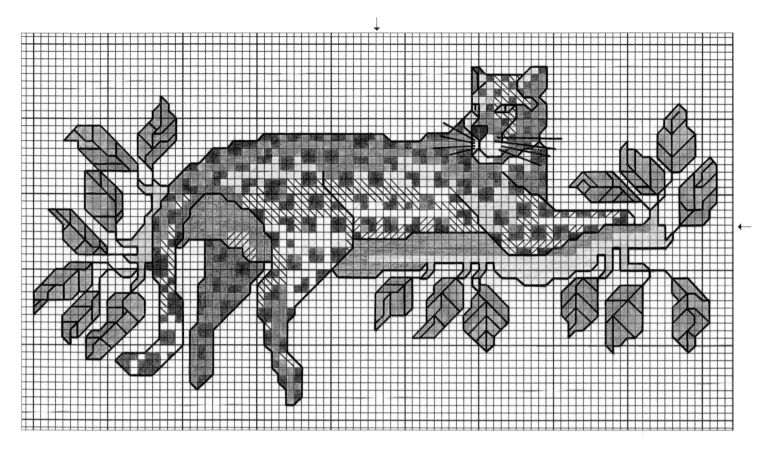

on your Aida fabric (see page 101). Work the cross stitches with two strands of embroidery thread. When you have completed the cross stitching, sew the outline of the leopard and tree trunk in back stitch, using one strand of DMC 310/Anchor 403. Still with this cotton, sew the whiskers in long stitch. Sew round the leaves in back stitch, using one strand of DMC 890/Anchor 1044.

To treat the finished embroidery, see page 101.

DMC	Anchor
310	403
822	390
744	305
436	901
761	1021
B5200	1
3072	847

DMC	Anchor
611	832
910	228
704	256
317	400
647	1040

Back stitch

DMC	Anchor
310	403
890	1044

Long stitch

DMC	Anchor
310	403

To make up the tie-back

Mark round the template on the lining fabric and both pieces of interfacing, and cut the three pieces out. Iron one piece of interfacing to the back of the Aida and the other to the back of the lining (referring to the interfacing for instructions). Place the two pieces of fabric right sides together, then pin, tack and machine stitch along the two long sides and one short end. Snip the corners diagonally to get rid of excess fabric, then turn right side out. Press. Tuck in the open end and over sew to close it.

Attach brass rings or cotton cord loops to each end and a hook to the required place on the wall or window frame.

Giraffe Lampshade

There are eight different types of giraffe, and wherever they come from in Africa, they like the freedom of wandering the vast grasslands.

Measurements
The finished embroidery size is 5 x 5cm (2 x 2in).

Materials
- Piece of antique white 16-count Zweigart DMC Aida measuring a good 5-8cm (2-3in) larger than the lampshade pattern (see below)
- DMC or Anchor stranded embroidery cotton, one skein of each colour shown on the chart
- Tapestry needle size 24-26
- 10cm (4in) embroidery hoop
- Simple lampshade
- Large piece of tracing paper for pattern
- PVA glue
- Cotton tape for binding edges
- Sewing machine or aerosol adhesive
- Basic sewing kit

To work the embroidery
Following the chart, start your embroidery from the centre of the markings you have placed on your Aida fabric (see page 101). Work the cross stitches with two strands of embroidery thread. When you have completed the cross stitching, sew the outline in back stitch, using one strand of DMC 310/Anchor 403, then use the same cotton to work French knots for the eye and horns. Finally, sew the grass in long stitch, using DMC 3345/Anchor 263.

To treat the finished embroidery, see page 101.

To make up the lampshade
Place your lampshade at one end of the piece of tracing paper. Mark where the seam line falls, then roll the shade right round until the seam is back on the paper, tracing the outline as you go. Add 1cm (⅜in) to each end and 2cm (¾in) to the top and bottom, then cut out.

Place the pattern on the Aida fabric, making sure it is centred over the design. (The tracing paper allows you to see the design's position.) Pin it in position, then mark and cut out the fabric. Fit the fabric over the lampshade, pinning the back seam to check for fit, then remove the shade and machine stitch down the seam; trim for a neat finish. Turn the lampshade cover to the right side, press, then put it back on the shade.

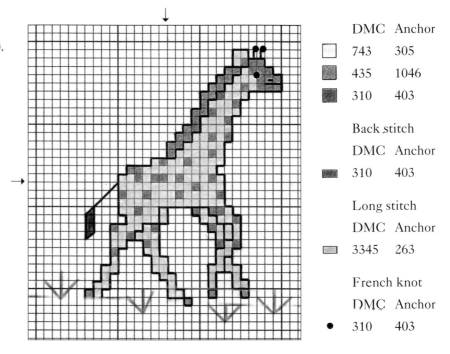

	DMC	Anchor
☐	743	305
▨	435	1046
▩	310	403

Back stitch

	DMC	Anchor
▬	310	403

Long stitch

	DMC	Anchor
▭	3345	263

French knot

	DMC	Anchor
●	310	403

Apply some glue to the top and bottom edges, fold them round to the inside of the shade, and press down firmly. You may have to snip into the raw edges at intervals to ensure a snug fit. Use clothes pegs to hold the fabric in place while it dries, if necessary. When the cover is dry, glue lengths of cotton tape round the inside of the shade at top and bottom to cover any raw edges and give a neat appearance. Leave to dry before using as a lampshade.

Another method of fitting the cover is to glue the fabric onto the shade. For this method, spray the reverse of the cut-out embroidered fabric with an aerosol adhesive, leave it to dry for a minute or two, then wrap the fabric round the shade, smoothing it firmly out to the edges. If the fabric is not flat, or is not quite in the right place, you can reposition it. When it is in place and as smooth as possible, turn under one of the edges at the back seam, then glue this edge down over the other one for a neat finish. Neaten the fabric at top and bottom as above.

CHILDREN'S ITEMS

The projects in this chapter are an ideal way to encourage children to learn about the geographical areas that animals come from. Many of these birds and animals are fast disappearing from our planet, and these fun embroidered items will remind children of the special place that our wildlife has on the earth.

Parrot Mobile

Parrots' beaks are well adapted to cracking open the nuts they feed on from the trees growing in tropical rain forests.

Measurements

The finished embroidery sizes are as follows:
Crimson rosella 13.3 x 5.3cm (5¼ x 2⅛in)
Gold and blue macaw 16 x 6.5cm (6⅜ x 2½in)
Rainbow lorikeet 10 x 5.5cm (4 x 2¼in)
Musk lorikeet 12.5 x 5.5cm (5 x 2¼in)
Golden conure 12 x 6.5cm (4¾ x 2½in)

Materials

- Piece of red 14-count Zweigart DMC Aida sufficient to fit in five pieces each measuring 18 x 25.5cm (7 x 10in)
- DMC or Anchor stranded embroidery cotton, one skein of each colour shown on the charts
- Tapestry needle size 24-26
- 15cm (6in) embroidery hoop
- Wadding to fill each parrot
- 3.7m (4yd) of 1cm (⅜in) wide red satin ribbon
- 51cm (20in) length of bamboo
- 15 small silver bells
- PVA glue
- Sewing machine
- Basic sewing kit

To work the embroidery

Centre the parrot designs on each measured piece of Aida (see page 101). Following the relevant chart, start embroidering your first parrot from the centre of these markings. Work the cross stitches with two strands of thread. When the cross stitch-

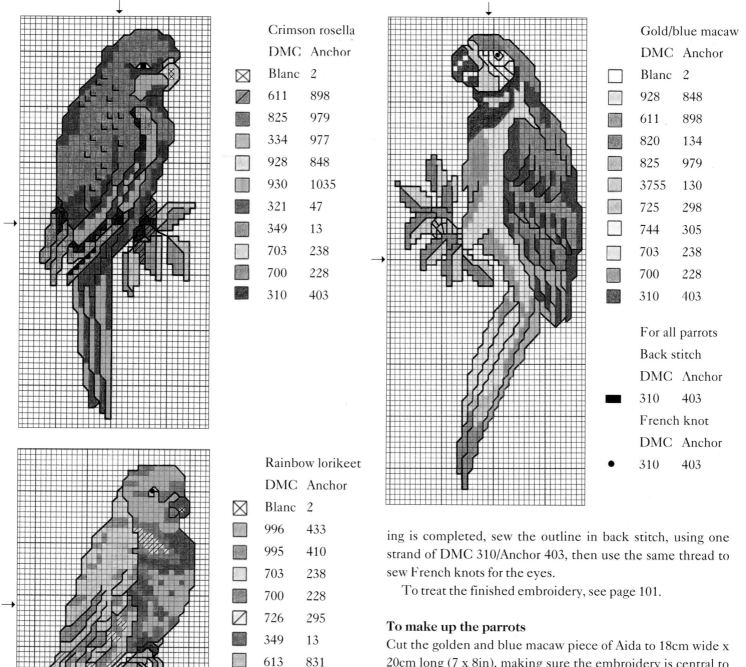

Crimson rosella

	DMC	Anchor
⊠	Blanc	2
⧅	611	898
▨	825	979
▨	334	977
▢	928	848
▨	930	1035
▨	321	47
▨	349	13
▢	703	238
▨	700	228
▨	310	403

Gold/blue macaw

	DMC	Anchor
▢	Blanc	2
▢	928	848
▨	611	898
▨	820	134
▨	825	979
▨	3755	130
▨	725	298
▢	744	305
▨	703	238
▨	700	228
▨	310	403

For all parrots
Back stitch

	DMC	Anchor
▬	310	403

French knot

	DMC	Anchor
●	310	403

Rainbow lorikeet

	DMC	Anchor
⊠	Blanc	2
▢	996	433
▨	995	410
▢	703	238
▨	700	228
⧅	726	295
▨	349	13
▨	613	831
▨	608	332
▨	310	403

ing is completed, sew the outline in back stitch, using one strand of DMC 310/Anchor 403, then use the same thread to sew French knots for the eyes.

To treat the finished embroidery, see page 101.

To make up the parrots
Cut the golden and blue macaw piece of Aida to 18cm wide x 20cm long (7 x 8in), making sure the embroidery is central to the cut fabric. Cut the other four parrots to 18 x 18cm (7 x 7in), again centring the embroidery.

Fold each parrot in half lengthwise, right sides together, and sew up the centre back seam, leaving a 1cm (⅜in) seam allowance. Adjust the fabric so that the seam lies at the centre

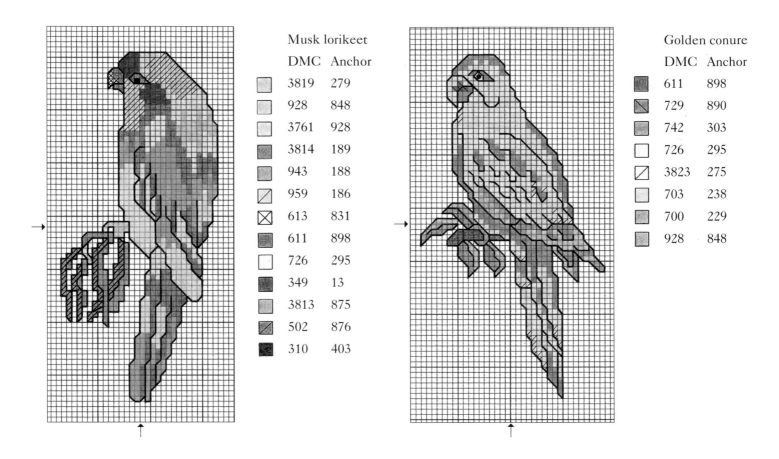

Musk lorikeet

DMC	Anchor
3819	279
928	848
3761	928
3814	189
943	188
959	186
613	831
611	898
726	295
349	13
3813	875
502	876
310	403

Golden conure

DMC	Anchor
611	898
729	890
742	303
726	295
3823	275
703	238
700	229
928	848

back, and sew across the bottom. Trim the seams and turn each parrot to the right side through the top open end. Stuff each parrot with wadding.

Cut the ribbon into six pieces, each measuring 61cm (24in). Pin one end of each length of ribbon to the right side of a centre back seam, so that the ribbon lies over the seam and its end aligns with the top of the fabric; keep in place with a couple of rows of machine stitching. Fold in the top raw edge, including the end of the ribbon, and pin, tack and machine top stitch into position. The ribbon should now be hanging from the top of each parrot.

To assemble the mobile
Glue the ends of the ribbons onto the bamboo, spacing the parrots evenly and grading the length of ribbons, working out from the centre: the macaw should hang the lowest in the centre (ribbon length 53cm/21in), the next two at 38cm (15in) and the next two at 25cm (10in).

Tie the sixth length of ribbon, from which the mobile will hang, across the width of the bamboo, leaving it a little slack and knotting it at either side of the two end parrots; glue down the ends of the knots for extra security. Finally, sew three bells on the bottom end of each parrot.

Note: if you have babies or young children, it would be wise either to omit the bells (which could cause choking) or to hang the mobile out of reach of tiny hands.

Bear Finger Puppet

The smallest bear in North America is the black bear. These bears are very agile and will climb trees to avoid danger.

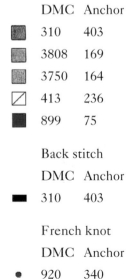

Measurements
The finished embroidery size is 7.5 x 4cm (3 x 1½in).

Materials
- Piece of white 14-count Zweigart DMC Aida measuring 20 x 15cm (8 x 6in)
- DMC or Anchor stranded embroidery cotton, one skein of each colour shown on the chart
- Tapestry needle size 24-26
- 10cm (4in) embroidery hoop
- Sewing machine
- Basic sewing kit

To work the embroidery
Centre the bear design at the lower end of the length of Aida as suggested on page 101. Following the chart, start working from the centre of these markings. Work the cross stitches with two strands of thread. When you have completed the cross stitching, sew round the bear and the markings on its face in back stitch, using one strand of DMC 310/Anchor 403. Work French knots for the eyes, using two strands of DMC 920/Anchor 340.

To treat the finished embroidery, see page 101.

To make up the finger puppet
Mark out round the embroidery a shape roughly 19cm (7½in) long by 7cm (2¾in) wide. Cut it out and zig zag round the raw edges to prevent them fraying.

Turn under and machine stitch a hem at the bottom of the strip about three squares down from the bottom of the bear's foot, and also one at the top. Turn under the side hems about two squares out from the sides of the bear, and tack in place. Fold the embroidered Aida strip in half; pin, tack and machine top stitch the folded side seams together to make the finger shape. The embroidery should be on one side and the other side should be plain.

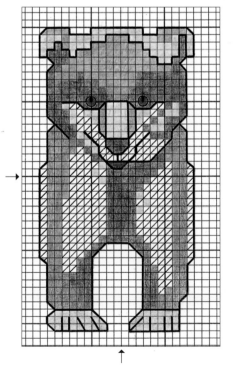

	DMC	Anchor
	310	403
	3808	169
	3750	164
	413	236
	899	75

Back stitch
	DMC	Anchor
	310	403

French knot
	DMC	Anchor
•	920	340

Polar Bear Hot Water Bottle Cover

These powerful white creatures must be an awesome sight to see wandering across the snowy landscape of the Arctic.

Measurements

The finished embroidery size is 14 x 8cm (5½ x 3⅛in).

Materials

- Piece of 14-count Zweigart DMC waste canvas measuring 20 x 15cm (8 x 6in)
- Piece of tear-away interfacing to the same size as the waste canvas
- DMC or Anchor stranded embroidery cotton, one skein of each colour shown on the chart

- Tapestry needle size 24-26
- 20cm (8in) embroidery hoop
- Piece of blue cotton fabric, pale blue cotton fabric and interlining, each measuring 76 x 50cm (30 x 20in)
- Piece of natural cord, 76cm (30in) long
- Sewing machine
- Basic sewing kit

To work the embroidery

Draw round a hot water bottle, up to the neck,

DMC	Anchor
B5200	1
B5200	1
800	120
809	121
3807	122
823	152

Back stitch

DMC	Anchor
823	152

French knot

DMC	Anchor
823	152

adding on 4cm (1½in) all round to allow for expansion and an easy fit. Shape the shoulders for a smooth outline. Pin this template onto the piece of blue fabric and mark out the shape. Cut away the remaining fabric roughly, but do not cut round the marked out shape yet. Centre the design by tacking in the central lines on both the fabric and the waste canvas, and matching the markings together. I started the design 11cm (4⅜in) from the bottom of the fabric. See page 101 for directions on waste canvas embroidery.

Following the chart, start your embroidery from the centre of the markings you have placed on your waste canvas (see page 101). Work the cross stitches with two strands of embroidery thread. When you have completed the cross stitching, sew the outline in back stitch, using one strand of DMC 823/Anchor 152, then use the same thread to work the French knots.

To treat the finished waste canvas embroidery, see page 101.

To make up the hot water bottle cover
Refer to page 107 for full instructions.

Lemur Toy Bag

True lemurs are found only on the island of Madagascar; they live mainly off the fruit and leaves of the tamarind tree.

Measurements

The finished embroidery size is 17 x 14.5cm (6¾ x 5¾in).

Materials

- Piece of red 14-count Zweigart DMC Aida measuring 25.5 x 25.5cm (10 x 10in)
- DMC or Anchor stranded embroidery cotton, one skein of each colour shown on the chart
- Tapestry needle size 24-26
- 20cm (8in) embroidery hoop
- Piece of blue cotton fabric, 69 x 50cm (27 x 19½in)
- Piece of red lining, 81 x 50cm (31½ x 19½in)
- Piece of red cord, 81cm (31½in) long
- Sewing machine
- Basic sewing kit

To work the embroidery

Centre the lemur design on the square of Aida. Following the chart, start your embroidery from the centre of the markings you have made on the Aida (see page 101). Work the cross stitches with two strands of thread. When you have completed the cross stitching, sew the outline in back stitch, using one strand of DMC 310/Anchor 403, then use the same thread to sew the whiskers in long stitch.

To treat the finished embroidery, see page 101.

To make up the toy bag

Cut the piece of embroidered Aida to a rectangle measuring 21cm wide x 23cm long (8¼ x 9in), making sure the lemur is central; this will be the pocket. Cut a 61 x 50cm (24 x 19½in) rectangle from the blue fabric for the bag then cut two 28 x 4cm (11 x 1½in) strips from the remainder. Cut two rectangles from the red lining, one to the same size as the embroidered Aida and the other to the same size as the blue bag.

Place the Aida and its matching lining right sides together; pin, tack and sew all round, taking a 1.5cm (⅝in) seam, but leaving a gap of about 7cm (2¾in). Pull the pocket through the gap to the right side. Press then sew up the gap by hand.

Fold the blue fabric in half widthwise (i.e 30.5 x 50cm/12 x 19½in) and tack in this centre line. Centre the pocket on one half of the blue fabric, about 5cm (2in) up from the raw bottom edge, with the lemur facing the fold line and its feet pointing down the length of the bag; pin, tack and top stitch down.

Fold the bag in half at the tacking line, right sides together, and pin, tack and machine stitch along the bottom and up the side seam. Pull through to the right side and press. Attach the red lining following the instructions on page 106.

Fold in the two short ends of both blue fabric strips and top stitch down. Fold in both raw edges down the length of each strip by 1cm (⅜in). (It helps to press the folds down.) Pin into position, about 2cm (¾in) in from the width on either side and 7cm (2¾in) down from the top of the bag. Tack and sew close to the edge on either side of the casings. Use a safety pin to push the cord through both casings to finish the neck, then knot both ends of the cord.

	DMC	Anchor
◺	Blanc	2
▩	310	403
▨	3072	847
☐	3782	899
▨	722	324
▨	840	374

	DMC	Anchor
▨	3021	905
▨	703	238
▨	700	228

Back stitch

DMC	Anchor
▬ 310	403

Long stitch

DMC	Anchor
▬ 310	403

Chameleon Pencil Case

Chameleons can change colour so that they blend in with their surroundings.
They catch food on their long sticky tongues.

Measurements

The finished embroidery size is 11 x 5.5cm (4⅜ x 2¼in).

Materials

- Piece of red 14-count Zweigart DMC Aida measuring 33 x 28cm (13 x 11in)
- DMC or Anchor stranded embroidery cotton, one skein of each colour shown on the chart
- Tapestry needle size 24-26
- 15cm (6in) embroidery hoop
- Piece of red tartan lining, 47 x 28cm (18½ x 11in)
- Piece of 2.5cm (1in) wide red touch and close tape, 33cm (13in) long
- Sewing machine
- Basic sewing kit

To work the embroidery

Fold the Aida in half to make two 33 x 14cm (13 x 5½in) shapes. Centre the design on one half of the Aida, so that the feet are in the direction of the fold of the pencil case when made up. Following the chart, start your embroidery from the centre of the markings you have made on the Aida (see page 101). Work the cross stitches with two strands of embroidery thread. When you have completed the cross stitching, sew the outline in back stitch, using one strand of DMC 310/Anchor 403. Use the same thread to work French knots for the eyes and the markings on the back.

To treat the finished embroidery, see page 101.

To make up the pencil case

Cut the lining to the same size as the Aida. Cut

DMC	Anchor
646	8581
721	324
743	305
703	238
3812	188
910	229

Back stitch

DMC	Anchor
310	403

French knot

DMC	Anchor
310	403

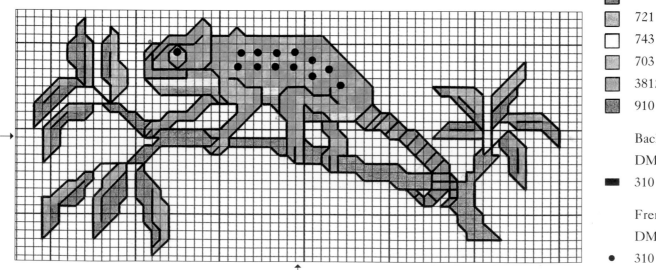

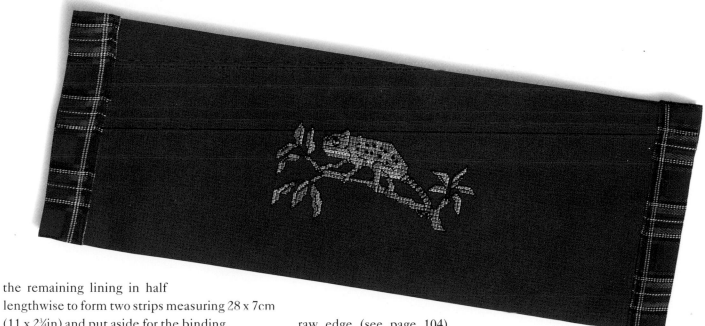

the remaining lining in half
lengthwise to form two strips measuring 28 x 7cm
(11 x 2¾in) and put aside for the binding.

Place the main piece of the lining and the Aida
right sides together; pin, tack and machine stitch
along both long edges, taking a 1.5cm (⅝in) seam.
Pull through to the right side and press to flatten.
Pin and tack the separate parts of the touch and
close tape to the right side of the lining down both
long sides (i.e. along the seams). Machine stitch
both parts into position at top and bottom.

Turn the pencil case over so that the embroidery is facing up, and apply a binding strip to each
raw edge (see page 104).
(The binding will extend beyond the top and bottom of the pencil case: fold the extra fabric over to
the lining side of the pencil case to neaten the
corners and tack into position.)

When the binding is stitched in place, fold the
pencil case in half, with the embroidery on the
outside, matching the two sides of the touch and
close tape to close. Machine top stitch down both
sides of the pencil case to secure, sewing on the
inside edge of the binding.

Koala Bear Playing Card Case

Koalas live in the eucalyptus forests of eastern Australia. They lead a solitary existence, or else group together in small harems led by a male.

Measurements

The finished embroidery size is 8 x 7cm (3¼ x 2¾in).

Materials

• Piece of grey 16-count Zweigart DMC Aida measuring 33.5 x 17cm (13¼ x 6⅝in) (Note: this case fits two packs of standard playing cards. If your cards are larger than average, you will need to adjust the amounts of fabric accordingly.)

• DMC or Anchor stranded embroidery cotton, one skein of each colour shown on the chart

• Tapestry needle size 24-26

• 10cm (4in) embroidery hoop

• Piece of lining fabric to the same size as the Aida

• Two packs of standard playing cards

• Piece of twisted cord, 28cm long (11in), bought or homemade (see page 104)

• Sewing machine

• Basic sewing kit

To work the embroidery

Zig zag all round the Aida to stop the edges from fraying. Measure up 2cm (¾in) from one of the 17cm (6⅝in) ends: that is the position of the bottom of the koala design, on the outside flap of the card case. Find the centre of the design from that point. Following the chart, start your embroidery from the centre of the markings you have made on the Aida (see page 101). Work the cross stitches with two strands of thread. When you have completed the cross stitching, sew the outline in back stitch, using one strand of DMC 310/Anchor 403, then use the same thread to work French knots for the eyes.

To treat the finished embroidery, see page 101.

To make up the card case

Assemble the layers of the card case following the instructions on page 105. Fold the plain end of the case about 9cm (3½in) up, lining sides together. Tack down the side edges and place the two packs of cards inside to check for fit. Machine top stitch the sides close to the edge. This makes the case to hold the cards. Place the two packs of cards inside to check for size and fold the embroidered flap over the top. Find the mid point of the flap and mark with a pin on the lining side. This is the position of the cord. Fold the cord in half, knot the ends and sew to the underside of the flap, where the pin is. Make a buttonhole loop (big enough to pass the knot of the cord through) at the bottom edge of the card holder to tie the cord through. (See page 102 for making a buttonhole loop and page 104 for making a twisted cord.)

DMC	Anchor
310	403
368	215
501	977
745	301
739	885
758	868
3765	169
611	898

DMC	Anchor
3072	847
300	352
841	373

Back stitch

DMC	Anchor
310	403

French knot

DMC	Anchor
310	403

Camel Trinket Box

The sturdy, double-humped Bactrian camel, bred to carry heavy loads, is able to stand colder climates than the single-humped Arabian camel.

Measurements

The finished embroidery size is 5 x 4cm (2 x 1½in).

Materials

- Piece of red 14-count Zweigart DMC Aida measuring 15 x 15cm (6 x 6in) (or a little larger than the box lid)
- DMC or Anchor stranded embroidery cotton, one skein of each colour shown on the chart
- Tapestry needle size 24-26
- 10cm (4in) embroidery hoop
- Small plain wooden box
- Thick wadding to the size of box lid
- PVA glue
- Bright paint (and paintbrush) or fabric to cover outside and inside of box
- Felt or braid to fit round lid and top edge of box
- Felt to cover box base
- Basic sewing kit

To work the embroidery

Centre the camel design on the Aida in a position that suits the box. Following the chart, start your embroidery from the centre of the markings you have made on the Aida (see page 101). Work the cross stitches with two strands of thread. When you have completed the cross stitching, sew the outline of the camel in back stitch, using two strands of DMC 310/Anchor 403, then sew the grass in long stitch, using two strands of DMC 910/Anchor 228.

To treat the finished embroidery, see page 101.

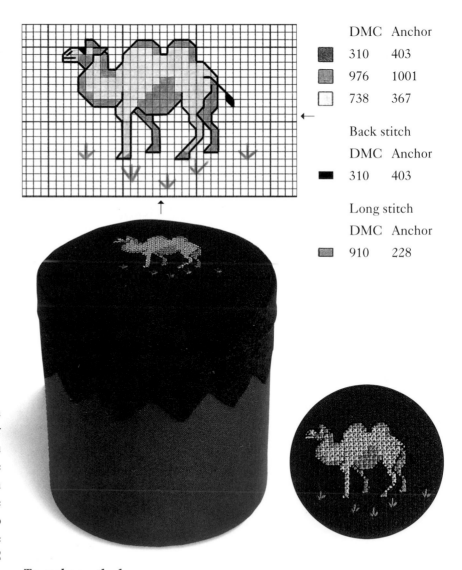

	DMC	Anchor
▨	310	403
▧	976	1001
☐	738	367

Back stitch

	DMC	Anchor
▬	310	403

Long stitch

	DMC	Anchor
▤	910	228

To make up the box

Refer to page 106 for full instructions.

Turtle Bookmark

These green turtles nest on the sandy beaches of the Florida Keys and swim in the clear blue waters surrounding these islands.

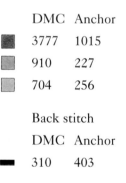

Measurements

The finished embroidery size is 11 x 2cm (4⅜ x ¾in).

Materials

- Piece of 14-count Zweigart DMC waste canvas measuring 2cm (¾in) larger all round than the bookmark template
- Piece of tear-away interfacing to the same size as the waste canvas
- DMC or Anchor stranded embroidery cotton, one skein of each colour shown on the chart
- Tapestry needle size 24-26
- 15cm (6in) embroidery hoop
- Bookmark template (see page 110) and some card
- Piece each of yellow and red felt, 25.5 x 25.5cm (10 x10in)
- Yellow embroidery machine thread (Madeira rayon 1024)
- Sewing machine
- Basic sewing kit

To work the embroidery

Trace the template on page 110 and transfer the outline onto the card. Mark the central vertical and horizontal lines onto the bookmark pattern. The centre will be the starting point for the embroidery. With a fabric marker, mark the card pattern onto the yellow felt, but do not cut it out yet. Mark the central lines of the bookmark across the piece of felt with tacking cotton.

Trace round the bookmark pattern onto the waste canvas and mark the central lines with the fabric marker. Lay the waste canvas on top of the felt, matching the central lines. See page 101 for directions on waste canvas embroidery.

Following the chart, start your embroidery from the centre of your markings on the waste canvas (see page 101). Work the cross stitches with two strands of embroidery thread. When you have completed the cross stitching, work one French knot for each eye, using one strand of DMC 310/Anchor 403, then use the same thread to outline the turtles in back stitch.

To treat the finished waste canvas embroidery, see page 101.

To make up the bookmark

Refer to page 107 for full instructions.

DMC	Anchor
3777	1015
910	227
704	256

Back stitch

DMC	Anchor
310	403

French knot

DMC	Anchor
310	403

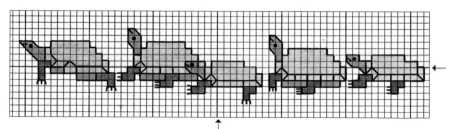

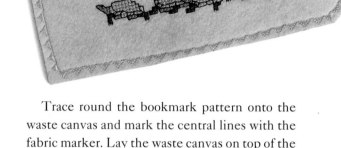

Chipmunk Pouch

Chipmunks put their food in pouches in their cheeks to carry back to their burrows. These stores will last them through their winter hibernation.

Measurements
The finished embroidery size is 7 x 6.5cm (2¾ x 2½in).

Materials
• Piece of beige 18-count Zweigart DMC Floba measuring 44 x 18cm (17½ x 7in)
• DMC or Anchor stranded embroidery cotton, one skein of each colour shown on the chart
• Tapestry needle size 24-26
• 10cm (4in) embroidery hoop
• Piece of lining fabric to the same size as the Floba
• Sewing machine
• Basic sewing kit

To work the embroidery
Sew zig zag stitch all round the raw edges to stop the fabric fraying. Measure down 18cm (7in) from the top and tack across the width of the fabric at this point. This is the fold line for the bottom of the pouch. Centre the embroidery in this area so that the chipmunk's head starts about 7cm (2¾in) down from the raw edges of the pouch and the tail ends about 4.5cm (1¾in) up from the tacked fold line. Following the chart, start your embroidery from the centre of the markings you have made on the Floba (see page 101). Work the cross stitches with one strand of thread. When you have completed the cross stitching, sew the outline in back stitch, using one strand of DMC 310/Anchor 403, then use the same thread to sew

the whiskers in long stitch. Sew the grass in long stitch, using two strands of DMC 704/Anchor 256.

To treat the finished embroidery, see page 101.

To make up the pouch
At the opposite end of the bag, measure down 7.5cm (3in) from the raw edge and tack in the fold line of the top of the pouch; this area makes the flap. Place the lining and the embroidered fabric right sides together, and pin, tack and machine stitch the two ends of both pieces of fabric together, leaving a 1.5cm (⅝in) seam allowance. Turn through to the right side and press the two layers of fabric to neaten. Zig zag stitch the two layers together, down the sides of the pouch.

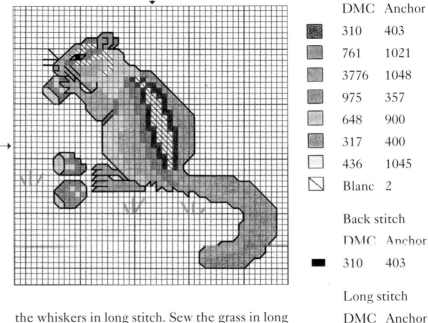

	DMC	Anchor
	310	403
	761	1021
	3776	1048
	975	357
	648	900
	317	400
	436	1045
	Blanc	2

Back stitch

	DMC	Anchor
	310	403

Long stitch

	DMC	Anchor
	310	403
	704	256

Choose a belt to use with this pouch, and machine stitch two buttonholes at the back of the pouch large enough for the belt to pass through, about 1.5cm (⅝in) down from the flap tacking line (the top end of the pouch) and 5cm (2in) in from the sides.

Following the tacked fold lines, fold the pouch into position so that the flap lies on top of the front of the pouch. The bottom of the flap should be about 1.5cm (⅝in) above the chipmunk's head. Pin and tack the sides of the flap to the top front of the pouch. Pull the bag wrong side out through one of the open side seams. Tack down both side seams, catching in the sides of the flap as well, using the tacked fold lines as a guide for positioning. Machine stitch down the sides, trim and turn through to the right side. Press to neaten and pass the belt through the buttonholes at the back of the pouch so that it can be worn round the waist.

Raccoon Cushion Cover

Some raccoons have escaped from zoos, and they are spreading throughout Europe, adapting to a lifestyle similar to that of the fox.

Measurements

The finished embroidery size is 12.5 x 13cm (5 x 5¼in).

Materials

- Piece of royal blue 14-count Zweigart DMC Aida measuring 25.5 x 25.5cm (10 x 10in)
- DMC or Anchor stranded embroidery cotton, one skein of each colour shown on the chart
- Tapestry needle size 24-26
- 15cm (6in) embroidery hoop
- Plain cushion cover
- Cushion pad to fit cover
- Basic sewing kit

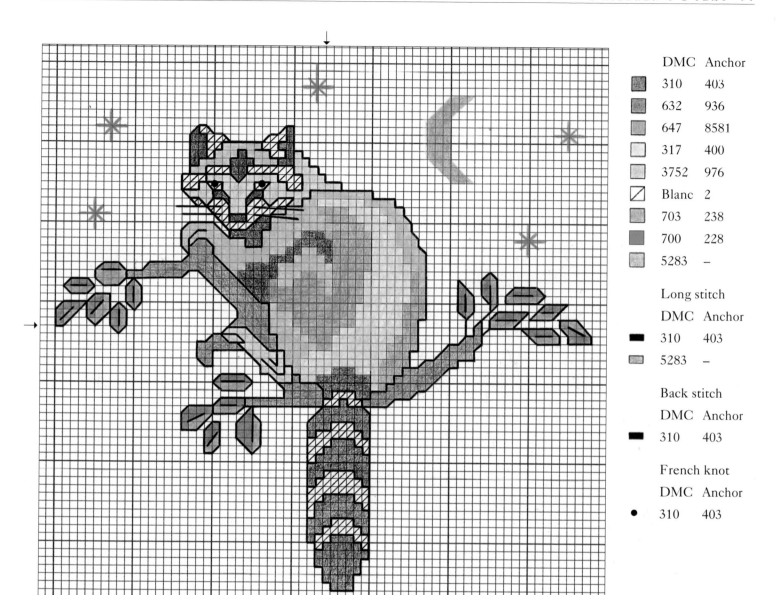

DMC	Anchor
310	403
632	936
647	8581
317	400
3752	976
Blanc	2
703	238
700	228
5283	–

Long stitch

DMC	Anchor
310	403
5283	–

Back stitch

DMC	Anchor
310	403

French knot

DMC	Anchor
310	403

To work the embroidery

Following the chart, start your embroidery from the centre of the markings you have made on the Aida (see page 101). Work the cross stitches with one strand of thread. When you have completed the cross stitching, sew the outline in back stitch, using one strand of DMC 310/Anchor 403, then use the same thread to stitch the whiskers in long stitch and to work French knots for the eyes.

Finally, sew long stitch for the stars and back stitch for the outline of the moon, using two strands of DMC 5283.

To treat the finished embroidery, see page 101.

To appliqué the design

Centre the raccoon on the front of the cushion cover, turning in the raw edges of the embroidered Aida. Pin, tack and top stitch it down.

MATERIALS AND TECHNIQUES

In this section you will find a list of the materials you'll need,
advice on different stitches, making-up instructions for some
of the projects plus a selection of templates to help you
reproduce the designs accurately.

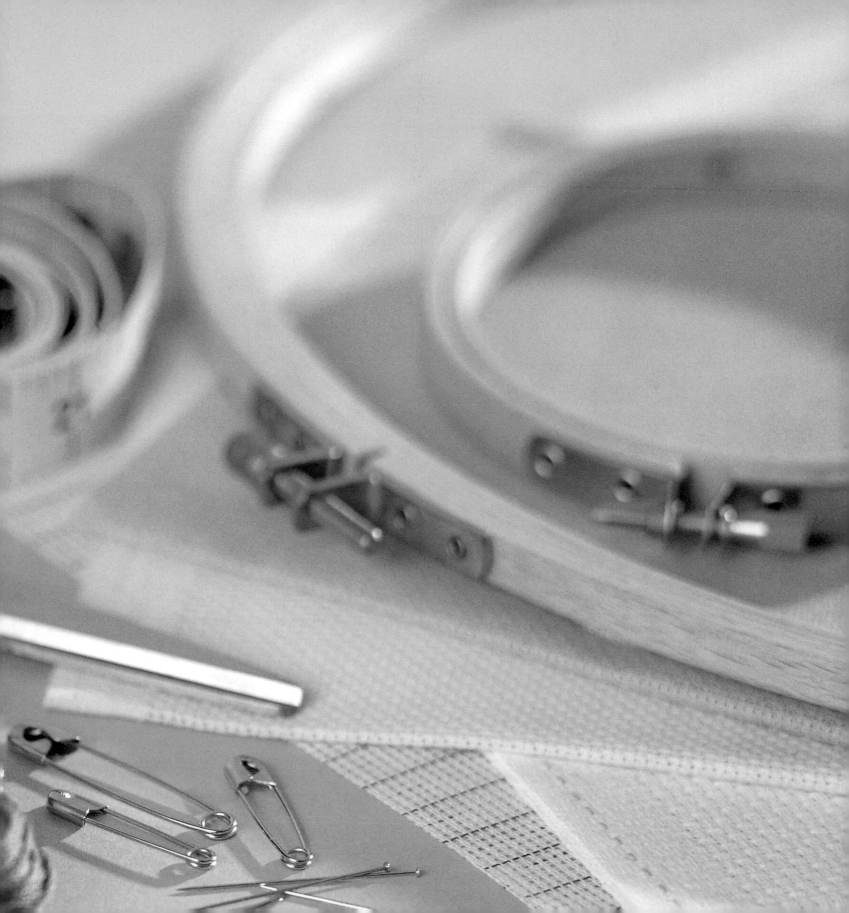

Basic Equipment

Fabrics

To make a perfect square with the cross stitch, you need to use an evenweave fabric. Evenweave means it has the same number of threads woven into it vertically (warp) as well as horizontally (weft), and is the easiest fabric to work with for cross stitch embroidery. Most of the projects in this book use Aida or waste canvas, though a few use Floba, which is a softer fabric that drapes well, making it suitable for items of clothing.

Aida comes in various colours and various counts. The count of a fabric refers to how many square blocks there are per 2.5cm (1in). Aida varies from 8 to 18 count. The higher the count, the smaller the embroidery will be. To prevent the fabric from fraying, oversew by machine with a zig zag stitch, or apply masking tape round the edges of the fabric.

Waste canvas is a fabric that allows you to embroider directly onto most materials that do not have a grid to work on, e.g. felt, denim, cotton, fine wool, fleece, etc. It comes in a range of counts from 8 to 14. By tacking this gridded canvas on top of the fabric, it is possible to work the cross stitch design easily, and the use of tear-away interfacing underneath the fabric stabilizes the embroidery. To use waste canvas, position the canvas on top of the fabric that you wish to embroider and place the interfacing underneath to make a sandwich. Embroider the design through all three layers. When you have finished, trim the waste canvas carefully round the finished embroidery, leaving a little margin, then moisten the canvas and carefully pull out the canvas threads with tweezers, leaving just the cross stitch design. Cut or tear away the interfacing from underneath the embroidery

Embroidery hoops

Although it is possible to work your design while holding the fabric in the hand, it is far more satisfactory to use a hoop. Embroidery hoops keep the work taut and the stitches neat. They consist of two rings, one smaller than the other. To fix the fabric onto the hoop, stretch the fabric over the smaller ring and then place the larger ring over the top and screw it tight to keep the fabric in position. To protect the fabric from being marked by the hard edge of the smaller ring, it is wise to wind strips of fabric round the ring. Hoops come in a range of sizes from 10cm (4in) to 30cm (12in).

Needles

Tapestry needles have large eyes for easy threading and blunt points that will not separate and split the fabric threads. A size 24-26 needle is suitable for all the projects in this book.

Threads

Several different types of thread are suitable for cross stitch. The ones used for the projects in this book are DMC stranded embroidery cotton, for which an equivalent colour code is given for Anchor yarns. These fine cottons come in a small skein and consist of six fine strands of thread, loosely twisted together. This enables you to cut off the length of thread needed and to use as many strands as specified for each project. Basically, 14- to 16-count Aida use two strands, whilst 18- to 20- use one. You can vary the texture of your embroidery through experimenting with different numbers of strands.

Basic sewing kit

For most of the projects in this book you will need the following basic sewing kit. Where a sewing machine is required, this is specified in the project introduction.

- Paper scissors
- Fabric scissors
- Embroidery scissors
- Tape measure
- Different coloured threads
- Variety of sewing needles
- Lots of sewing pins
- Unpicker
- Thimble
- Various sized safety pins
- Tweezers
- Tracing paper for patterns
- Fabric marker
- Tailor's chalk

How to Cross Stitch

To centre a cross stitch design

For each project, the embroidery position will vary according to the design of the object, but whatever the project and wherever you decide to place the design, the centring method is the same. Always remember to leave plenty of space around the embroidery, particularly in the case of small items that might otherwise not fit an embroidery hoop.

Refer to the coloured cross stitch chart that accompanies each project and check the dimensions of each design given alongside. Find the centre point of the design with the aid of the arrows marked on two sides of the chart. From the vertical arrow, trace a straight line downwards through the chart to the bottom; from the horizontal arrow, trace another straight line across through the chart to the other side. Where they intersect marks the centre of the design.

To centre the design on the Aida fabric, fold it in half both ways, making a crease line; the resulting intersection of the two lines is the centre of the design. Tack in the two lines in a contrasting thread. Correspond the centre of the chart with the centre of the marked fabric and begin to sew at this point. If the design is not to be placed centrally, work out the approximate area in which it will be placed from the project instructions, then mark the vertical and horizontal halfway lines of this area.

To embroider on waste canvas

If you are working with waste canvas, tack in the central design lines on the fabric you are using, in the same way as for the Aida. Since you cannot fold the stiff waste canvas, refer to the measurements given in each project for the dimensions of the finished design and use these as a guide. Your stitching area must be greater than these dimensions, and you must allow a margin for fixing the hoop. Establish a boundary for the design, and divide the designated area into equal quarters by marking vertical and horizontal lines with a fabric marker or with tacking stitches in a contrasting thread. They cross at the mid-point of the canvas. Repeat to mark the mid-point of the

piece of interfacing. Use the tacking lines to line up all three mid-points of the waste canvas, the fabric and the interfacing. Secure all three layers together with firm tacking before starting to stitch.

To work the cross stitch

Each project is accompanied by one chart and each square on the chart represents one cross stitch. The coloured squares in the chart correspond to the relevant key and the numbers in the key indicate the colour codes for the yarns. Where there are blank squares in the surrounding design, leave the fabric plain. The arrows on two sides of the chart will help you to find the mid-point of the design.

Keep a careful count of the stitches as you work and follow the design accurately.

Once you have fixed the fabric centrally inside the embroidery hoop, start stitching in the middle of the design and work outwards. It is best to work each small area of one colour and then change the thread to the next colour to work the adjacent stitches. In this way there will be less mistakes than if you work all the stitches of one colour before changing thread.

You may like to use a ruler or a piece of card to mark off each area of the chart as you complete it; this will help you to concentrate on one area at a time.

To treat the finished embroidery

When you have completed the design and removed all the waste canvas and interfacing, if used, wash the finished item in warm water with a gentle soap powder to remove any dirt that has got onto it during stitching. Dry the cross stitch by rolling it up in a towel when it is still damp, then place the embroidery face down on a towel and press with an iron on a low setting on the wrong side of the fabric to flatten the finished work. Allow your work to dry thoroughly before mounting it or making it up into the finished item.

The Stitches

MACHINE STITCHING HINTS

Pressing the seams flat between each stage of machine stitching will make your work look much crisper. Trim excess seam allowances to relieve bulk in the seams.

Use the reverse stitch button to secure the beginning and end of each machine stitched line by starting to stitch about 1cm (⅜in) in from the edge and reversing to the edge before sewing forwards. This will stop the stitches from unravelling.

STARTING AND FINISHING YOUR CROSS STITCH

To start or finish your sewing, do not tie a knot as this will show as an unsightly bump on the finished embroidery and may eventually come undone and loosen the stitches in the design. Either secure the thread by sewing one or two back stitches in an area that will eventually be covered by the cross stitch design, or leave a tail of thread on the wrong side of your sewing that you can then catch up and hold fast in the back of the first few stitches. To secure a new thread and to finish a thread, slide the needle on the wrong side of the fabric under stitches already worked.

Back stitch Back stitch is used in cross stitch design to outline and highlight the design. Working from right to left, bring the needle up to the right side of the fabric and make a short backward stitch. With the needle now below the fabric, take a forward stitch to the left that is twice as long as the backward stitch. Continue inserting and bringing up the needle a stitch length behind and in front of the previous stitch. The stitches underneath will be twice the length of those on top.

Blanket stitch Work over a raw or folded edge to secure and to decorate, using a contrasting thread for emphasis. On the right side of the fabric, insert the needle at the required distance at right angles to the edge. Bring the needle up just behind the edge of the right side of the fabric, loop the thread behind the needle and pull the needle up in front of the thread to form the loop. Continue to form a series of loops along the edge. You can vary the size of the stitches.

Buttonhole loop A bar of straight stitches is sewn through the fabric (two to three stitches), as long as you would like the loop to be. Blanket stitch is then sewn close together over this bar of stitches to make the loop. Secure the loop properly on the wrong side of the fabric.

Buttonhole stitch This is used for neatening holes. Bring the needle up through the fabric at the required distance from the edge, then pass the needle down over the raw edge and back up just to the right of the original point, looping the thread under the needle as you pull it through. Continue in this way so that all the stitches lie close together.

Cross stitch You can work cross stitches in horizontal, vertical or diagonal rows. To fill in an area, it is best to work in horizontal rows. First work a number of diagonal stitches from right to left, then work back over the diagonal threads from left to right, so that each stitch forms a cross. If you are working diagonally and in small areas, it is better to complete each stitch before you begin the next one.

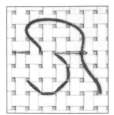

back stitch

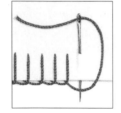

blanket stitch

buttonhole loop

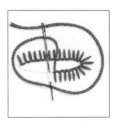

buttonhole stitch

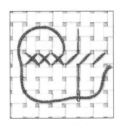

cross stitch

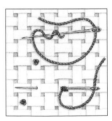

french knot

French knot A round raised stitch like a bobble, this is useful for representing eyes and flowers, etc. Bring the thread to the right side of the fabric where you want the knot to be. Twist the thread round the needle twice. Holding the thread firmly with your thumb, push the needle back down through the fabric in a position very near to where the needle first emerged. Hold the knot down with your thumb. Pull the thread through on the wrong side of the fabric and secure the knot with one or two small stitches. For a smaller knot, use just one twist; for a larger one, use three.

Half cross stitch A half cross stitch is a single diagonal line across the square to be filled, which complements full cross stitch. This is similar to tent stitch, but uses less thread and is more suitable when producing small-scale designs.

Long stitch This easy stitch is mainly used in this book for grass and for whiskers on animals. Each stitch can be as long as you wish and can go in any direction.

Oversewing Oversewing comprises a series of diagonal stitches on the wrong side of the fabric, and small catching stitches in the main fabric that barely show on the right side. Use as a form of hemming: turn under the raw edge of the hem allowance and oversew along the fold line, catching the main fabric with tiny stitches to secure the hem and to hide the raw edge.

Running stitch This consists of short stitches running in and out of the fabric in a single line. To ease the fabic into a gather, pull the threads at each end of a double row of running stitches with equal pressure.

Quarter cross stitch See Three-quarter cross stitch.

Tacking or basting These loose running stitches are longer on the right side of the fabric and shorter on the reverse side. Use a contrasting thread for a stitching a guideline, either to centre a design or to mark the path of a seam. Remove these stitches after sewing.

Tailor's tacks Use a contrasting double thread to make several loose loops through the pattern paper and the fabric; these form helpful and removable marks for lining up pattern pieces when making up some of the projects. Cut the thread between each stitch before removing the pattern, taking care not to remove the threads when pulling off the pattern. If you have stitched through two layers of fabric, ease both layers apart a little and snip the threads between them before removing the pattern, as above.

Three-quarter and quarter cross stitch Where squares are shown on the chart divided diagonally, with half the square in one colour and half in another, three-quarter and quarter cross stitches are needed. When a divided square is on the edge of the design, work a three-quarter cross stitch to fill the shaded area and leave the remaining quarter blank. When a square within the design is divided, stitch one part as a three-quarter stitch and the other as a quarter stitch.

Top stitch Top stitching produces a neat row of machine stitches visible on the right side of the fabric, for example on the edges of pockets and cord casings.

Zig zag stitch A zig zag machine stitch can be varied in length and width. Close together, the zig zag produces a satin stitch that can be used for decorative work. Wide apart, it can be used round raw edges as a quick way to stop fabric fraying.

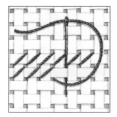
half cross stitch

long stitch

oversewing

tailor's tacks

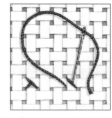
three-quarter stitch

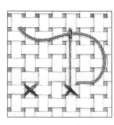
quarter stitch

Making-up Instructions

TWISTED CORD

Use several colours of the stranded cottons, each three times as long as the required length. Knot the strands together at each end and loop one end over a hook. Loop the other end over a pencil; then, holding the threads taut, twist the pencil round and round until the cord is so twisted that it is almost curling back on itself. Take hold of the centre and release both ends; it will twist itself together to form a thicker cord. Knot each end and cut the ends off neatly.

BIAS BINDING

These narrow strips of fabric are cut on the cross for binding raw edges. Find the true bias by folding the straight raw edge of your fabric so that it is parallel with the selvedge. Mark and cut out strips of fabric parallel to this diagonal line (1). Join strips by placing them at a right angle, right sides together, and stitching across the join (2). Press the bias in half lengthways, wrong sides together; open out, then turn in the raw edges so that they nearly meet in the middle. Press again. To apply the binding to a raw edge, open out the binding and lay it a little way in from the edge (3). Stitch along the fold line; turn the binding over to cover the edge, then oversew the other folded edge in place (4).

Bias binding is also available ready made in various colours.

TO MOUNT A CARD

Panda Card; Wapiti Deer Card

Open out the card, right side facing up. Place the embroidery underneath the oval frame to centre the design. Mark the correct position of the embroidery with a fabric marker just inside the centre folds, at top and bottom of the card. Turn the card over, right side facing down. Cut away any excess fabric to just a little smaller than the central panel of card.

Cover the area where the embroidery will be placed with a litle glue or double-sided sticky tape. Place the embroidered design into the glued position and press it down to fix. Glue inside the left-hand panel of the card and fold this over the wrong side of the embroidery to neaten. Press firmly to fix.

TO MOUNT A PICTURE

Siberian Tiger Picture; Four Tropical Fish Pictures; Pet Sampler

Cut a piece of acid-free backing board to fit your frame, and place this on the back of your embroidery. Secure it with masking tape on two facing sides. Using strong thread, lace the fabric edges together across the back of the board with a herringbone stitch, as shown right. Work out from the middle of each side, gently pulling the stitches taut, then repeat for the other two sides, first tucking in the corners neatly.

How to twist a cord

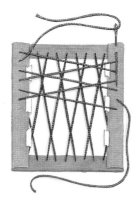

How to lace Aida together over a backing board

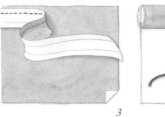

1 *2* *3* *4*

How to cut and join together strips of bias binding and then use them to neaten an edge

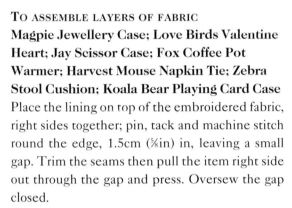

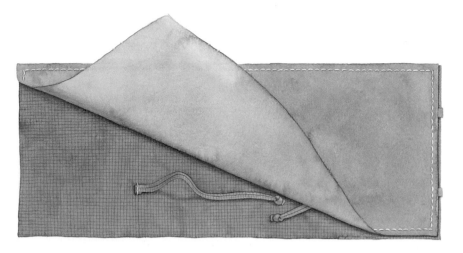

How to attach a lining, showing the positioning of ties and a frill

TO ASSEMBLE LAYERS OF FABRIC
Magpie Jewellery Case; Love Birds Valentine Heart; Jay Scissor Case; Fox Coffee Pot Warmer; Harvest Mouse Napkin Tie; Zebra Stool Cushion; Koala Bear Playing Card Case

Place the lining on top of the embroidered fabric, right sides together; pin, tack and machine stitch round the edge, 1.5cm (⅝in) in, leaving a small gap. Trim the seams then pull the item right side out through the gap and press. Oversew the gap closed.

If the project involves wadding, attach this to the reverse side of the embroidered piece by tacking round the outside, then proceed as above.

Some of the projects involve attaching a frill (see above, left), and others use ties (see above, right), both of which are inserted in the seam allowance and face inwards, with their edges aligned with those of the fabric. Frills and ties will need to be in place before you stitch the layers together round the edge, and in both cases they become the 'filling' in a sandwich of fabric.

TO FINISH THE BUTTERFLY PHOTOGRAPH FRAME
First, mark the central position of the embroidery with tacking thread, then turn the embroidery over to the wrong side. Using a fabric marker, lightly mark the position of the oval-shaped inner frame by counting the squares in from the embroidered border, matching it to the corresponding oval frame shape on the chart.

Tack over the marked line; the tacking will show through on the right side of the embroidery and so help the framer to position where the area of the photograph should be.

TO MAKE UP A LINED BAG
Dolphin Cotton Wool Bag; Octopus Pot Pourri Bag

Pin, tack and machine stitch the lining to the back of the embroidered Aida, 1.5cm (⅝in) from the top end of the bag (i.e. away from the design). Press the seam open.

Fold the bag in half lengthwise, inside out, to form a long tube. Pin, tack and machine stitch up the length of the bag, leaving a 1.5cm (⅝in) seam, starting from the bottom end of the lining, crossing the seam where the lining and Aida meet, and finishing 5cm (2in) down the Aida seam for the Dolphin, 3cm (1⅛in) for the Octopus (back stitching at this point for strength). Leave a gap of 1.5cm (⅝in) for the cord then carry on stitching (back stitching first for strength) down the rest of the Aida seam to finish. Press the seam open, placing it at the centre back of the bag.

For the Dolphin project, stitch across the

bottom of the Aida and turn the bag right side out. Poke out the corners of the bag with something pointed, then press to neaten. (For the Octopus project, refer back to the instructions on page 47.)

At this point the lining will be sticking out of the top end of the bag, with the raw edges of its bottom end showing. Turn the raw edges in towards the wrong side of the bag by 1.5cm (⅝in). Pin, tack and top stitch this seam near the edge to close the lining. Push the lining through to the inside of the bag, then press the top edge of the bag to neaten.

To make the cord channel, measure the distance of the hole down from the top edge of the bag (about 5cm/2in for the dolphin; 3cm/1⅛in for the octopus) and mark this distance all round with pins. Stitch round the bag, following these marks. Repeat this process below the hole. Attach a safety pin to one end of the cord then thread it though the casing

TO ATTACH A LINING TO A BAG
Armadillo String Bag; Lemur Toy Bag
Fold the lining in half, right sides together, and sew up the centre back seam. Do not turn to the right side; instead, slip this over the main fabric, right sides together and matching centre seams, and machine stitch the two top edges together.

Pull the lining up to the right side, and turn in the raw edges at the bottom. Pin, tack and machine stitch. Push the lining inside the bag.

TO MAKE UP THE MAGPIE JEWELLERY CASE
Trim the embroidered fabric to an oblong measuring 48 x 19cm (19 x 7½in).

Cut out four ties from the remaining Aida fabric, each measuring 23 x 4cm (9 x 1½in). Turn in both raw edges down the length of each tie, then pin, tack and top stitch down to secure. Pin then stitch the ties onto the case (see above for positions of ties).

Assemble the three layers of the jewellery case following the instructions on page 105. (Note that the ties attached to the flap will be sandwiched into the seam allowance.) Mark the fold lines onto the fabric with pins, then fold the fabric into the case shape. Top stitch down both sides of the case (but not the flap) to secure.

Finally, knot the ends of the ties and tie them together in pairs.

TO MAKE UP THE CAMEL TRINKET BOX
Spread adhesive over the top of the box lid and place the wadding on top. Press firmly all round. Glue round the edge of the lid, then place the embroidered fabric on top of the wadding and stick the fabric to the sides of the lid. Do not take the fabric round to the inside of the lid, or it will make the lid too bulky to fit over the box. Trim away the excess fabric round the bottom edge of the lid and leave to dry.

Paint the bottom part of the box, inside and out, but again leave the rim free for easy closure. Alternatively, you can cover the box with fabric, glued on, again leaving the rim free. To hide the raw edges of the embroidered fabric and to add interest to the box, glue felt or braid round the bottom of the lid (and also below the rim if the box is covered in fabric).

Fabric for Magpie Jewellery Case, showing fold lines and positions of ties

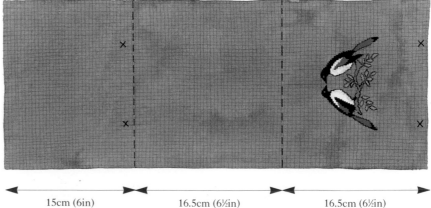

15cm (6in)   16.5cm (6½in)   16.5cm (6½in)

Finally, glue a piece of felt to the base of the box to hide any raw edges and to protect surfaces from being scratched.

To make up the Turtle Bookmark

Press the finished design the wrong way up on a towel. Cut away the excess felt around the bookmark, but leave a good 2cm (¾in) all round.

Mark the card pattern onto the red felt, then cut this out and use it as the backing for the bookmark. Pin and tack the red felt to the back of the embroidered piece. Use a decorative machine embroidery stitch to sew the two layers together, machining round the inside of the traced bookmark with the Madeira thread. Trim round the edge with a sharp pair of scissors, leaving 3mm (⅛in) clear of the machine stitch.

To finish, make a simple tassel about 5cm (2in) long, using the Madeira thread. Cut a strip of card about 5cm (2in) wide, and wind the cotton round it 40-50 times. Hold the threads at one end, and snip through at the other. Wind a threaded needle round the threads three or four times, about halfway up, then secure the thread by stitching it down through the bundle and snipping it off. Sew the tassel to the point of the bookmark.

To make up the Polar Bear Hot Water Bottle Cover

Cut out two hot water bottle pieces from the pale blue fabic, a further two from the interlining and one from the blue fabric. Cut round the marked out shape on the embroidered piece of fabric. Finally, cut out two lengths from the remaining blue fabric, each measuring 22.5 x 4cm (8¾ x 1½in) for the cord casing.

Place both pieces of interlining on the wrong side of the two blue pieces of fabric. Tack round the edge of each pair to keep the layers together. Now pin the two pale blue pieces to the blue ones, right sides together (i.e. on the side away

from the interlining). Pin, tack and machine stitch through all three layers round the top of both bottle shapes, from shoulder to shoulder. Trim the stitched area to within 3mm (⅛in).

Turn both pieces right sides out, so that the lining now covers the interlining, and press the curves to neaten them. Tack together the remaining raw edges of each three-layered piece.

Turn under a double 1.5cm (⅝in) hem at both ends of each piece of casing; press and stitch down. Turn under the long raw edges of each piece to produce two tubes, each 2cm (¾in) wide. Pin, tack and machine stitch in position to the outside of the two halves of the hot water bottle cover, 9cm (3½in) down from the top, leaving the ends free for the cord to run through.

Place the two halves of the cover together, right sides (i.e. blue fabric) facing. Pin, tack and machine stitch round all the raw edges, 1.5cm (½in) from the edge, starting about 2cm (¾in) above the raw edge at one shoulder and finishing the same distance above the raw edge at the other. Trim the raw edges to neaten, leaving about 6mm (¼in). Zig zag or overlock by machine or finish by hand.

Attach a safety pin to one end of the cord, then thread it through both lengths of casing. Cut the cord to the required length and knot the ends to stop them fraying.

How to assemble the pieces of the Polar Bear Hot Water Bottle Cover

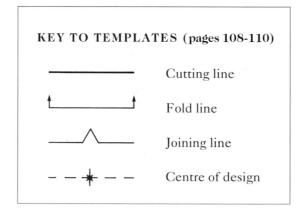

KEY TO TEMPLATES (pages 108-110)

————	Cutting line
↑———↑	Fold line
——⌃——	Joining line
– – ✳ – –	Centre of design

Templates

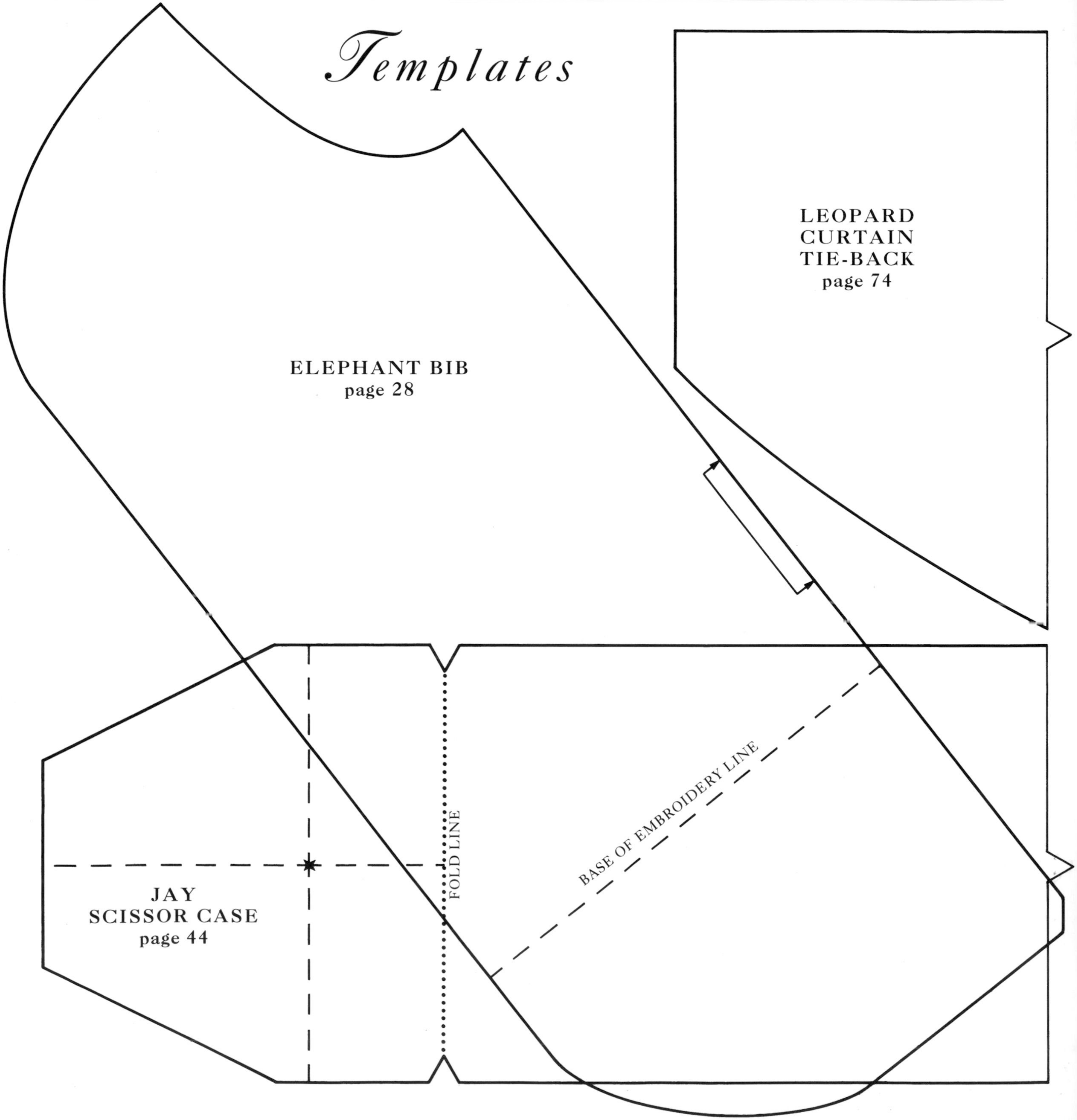

LEOPARD
CURTAIN
TIE-BACK
page 74

ELEPHANT BIB
page 28

JAY
SCISSOR CASE
page 44

FOLD LINE

BASE OF EMBROIDERY LINE

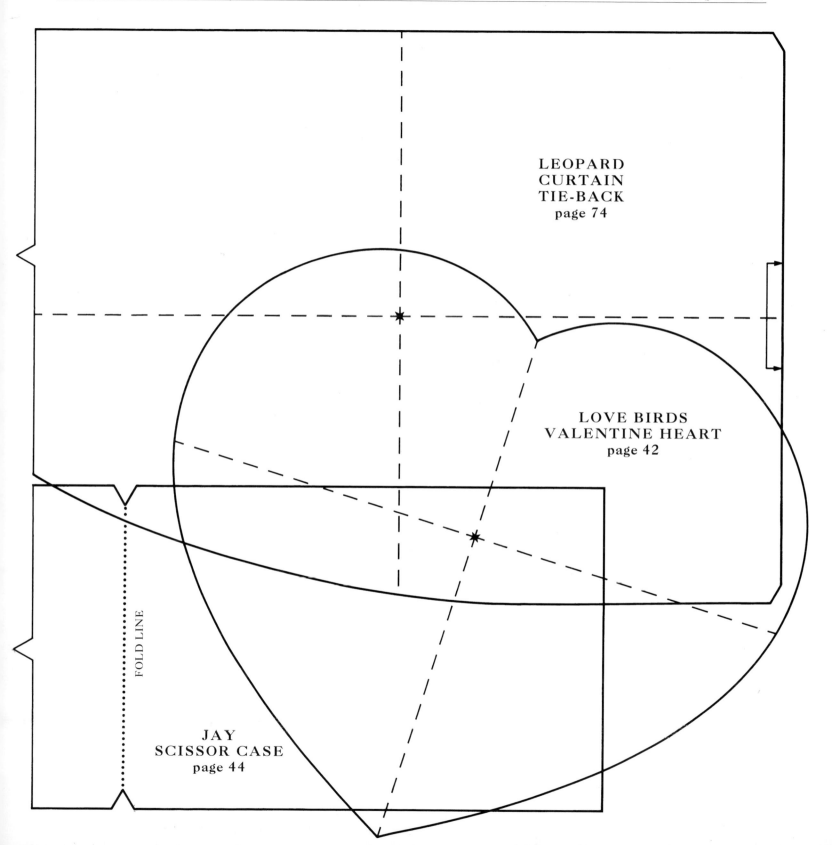

LEOPARD
CURTAIN
TIE-BACK
page 74

LOVE BIRDS
VALENTINE HEART
page 42

FOLD LINE

JAY
SCISSOR CASE
page 44

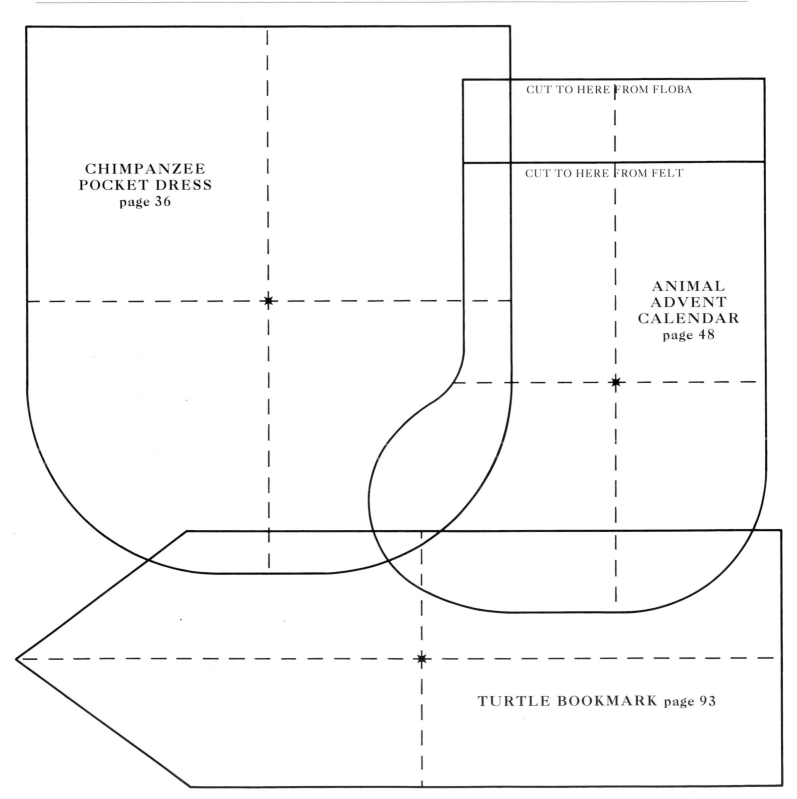

CHIMPANZEE
POCKET DRESS
page 36

CUT TO HERE FROM FLOBA

CUT TO HERE FROM FELT

ANIMAL
ADVENT
CALENDAR
page 48

TURTLE BOOKMARK page 93

Suppliers

UK

Coats Crafts UK
PO Box 22, The Lingfield Estate
McMullen Road
Darlington
County Durham DL1 1YQ
Tel : 01325 394394
(Suppliers of embroidery fabrics, Anchor threads and Kreinik metallic threads)

Craft Creations Ltd
Units 1-7
Harper's Yard
Ruskin Road
Tottenham
London N17 8QA
Tel : 0181 885 2655
Fax : 0181 808 0746
(Suppliers of card mounts, card, paper, packaging, picture mounts, etc. Orders accepted from abroad)

DMC Creative World
Pullman Road
Wigston
Leicester
Leicestershire   E18 2DY

USA

The DMC Corporation
Port Kearny
Building 10
South Kearny
New Jersey 070032

Coats and Clark
Greenville
South Carolina
(Anchor threads)

Joan Toggit Ltd
2 Riverview Drive
Somerset
New Jersey 08873
(Zweigart fabrics)

AUSTRALIA AND NEW ZEALAND

DMC
51-61 Carrington Road
Marrickville
New South Wales 2204

Warnaar Trading Co Ltd
376 Ferry Road
PO Box 19567
Christchurch
(DMC threads and Zweigart fabrics)

Coats Patons Crafts
Mulgrave 3170
Australia
(Anchor threads)

SOUTH AFRICA

SATC
43 Somerset Road
PO Box 3868
Capetown 800
(DMC threads)

Brasch Hobby
10 Loveday Street
PO Box 6405
Johannesburg 2000
(Zweigart fabrics)

NEEDLE PRODUCTS

All DMC and Anchor threads and Zweigart fabrics used in this book are available from the relevant stockists given below and many other needlecraft outlets the world over. The addresses given are the head offices or agents – contact them for advice on local availability of threads. Good haberdasheries should also supply other products, including embroidery hoops, cards, needles, scissors etc.

Index

ACKNOWLEDGEMENTS

A very special thank you to Wendy Cockburn, who has worked so hard, at all hours, embroidering all the projects for me in this book. Thanks also to Barbara Tremewan for helping with the computer and to Stephanie Chapman for making up items of clothing.

Special thanks to Alex Tai for supplying the animal illustrations (page 8) and Ronald Lew for making up the clotheshorse (page 22).